Infamous

Part 1

Michael Hendricks

ISBN: 978-1-09830-785-1

Library of Congress Control Number: 00000000000

Any references to historical events, real people, or real places are used fictitiously. Names, characters, and places are products of the author's imagination.

Book design by Carolyn Richardson

Printed by Bookbaby.com in the United States of America.

First printing edition 2020.

Michael Hendricks
c/o Roxell Richards & Associates
6420 Richmond Ave. Ste. #135
Houston, TX 77057

Dedication

This book is dedicated to my faithful attorney Roxell Richards. Thank you for all that you do on my behalf. To my little brother, Jay Jay, may he rest in peace. Hope you are dancing with the angels. To my mom Geraldine, thank you for giving me life. Thank you for all that you instilled in me: my drive and my passion. You inspired me in more ways than the world can imagine. Hope you're in heaven now with perfect wings. To my brother Greg: we weren't raised together, and although we share the same blood, we didn't share the same dreams. Still, it's all the same love. To my friends, thank you for the support. To my foes, thank you for the motivation. When you tried to stop me, I just went harder. When you said, I lacked game, I got smarter.

Prologue

"Johnson!" Hearing your name being called for release is the best feeling you can have in jail. "Johnson," the tall redneck officer calls again. "Right here," I answer, moving through the line of other anxious inmates waiting to be released. "If you want to go home hurry your ass up," he rushes. This sloppy-built muthafucker is sweating in the A/C. "Name," the releasing officer asks as I step to the desk and speak, "Johnson, 6031 West Airport, 5123542." They hand me the wallet, watch and cell phone I had when I was booked. But instead of the cash I had on me, they hand me a check instead.

"You can cash your check as you leave or at the store across the street," the officer says blankly. "No Shit Sherlock," I mumble, grabbing my stuff and leaving.

"I heard that smartass!" he fires back. To the left, I can cash my check and my exit is to the right. I make the left, and a recognizable face greets me.

"Lil 50?" I call out.

"Infamous," my long-time partner answers.

"Nigga wait for me outside, we gotta talk," I tell him before cashing my check. I notice the time is 12:30a.m., so I know the gypsy cabs are hustling right outside. I might catch some females waiting for rides too. I take a deep breath as I step into freedom, meeting Lil' 50 as we walk side-by-side.

I turn towards the building one last time, "Goodbye, Harris County!" I say to the not-so-luxurious county lock up. I hate downtown Houston 'cause the only time I come around is when I'm getting out of the county jail.

5

"Infamous," Lil 50 shouts, surprised to be in my presence.

"Damn nigga. I didn't know they popped you two, 50," I say looking over at my lil' homey. We call him Lil' 50 because he resembles the rapper. Just a little bit smaller.

"Nigga they caught me slippin' on them bars and drank," 50 explains. "I woke up in that bitch not knowing what the fuck had happened," he says with his heavy drawl.

"Man, you crashing like that my nigga," I say shaking my head. Slippers count and they always create an unnecessary set back.

"What happened to you then?" He asks frowning. "Oh, let me guess, Lil' Puss." He continues accurately.

"Fuck you!" I respond. Yeah, I have a crazy bitch in my life that's been brining me down. I been thinking about letting her go for a while now.

"Let me tell you what this bitch did." I say launching into the long story that is the latest reason for me being locked up. "Me and my boy Pat was at Sunrise Hotel on South Main. I had just cashed my check and did a re-up on some hard. This crazy bitch decided to lose her marbles on me and cause a scene in the fuckin' parking lot. Right at the same time my boy Pat was getting into it with a fucking crackhead."

"Wait," he stops me. "You mean to tell me yo' dumbass got popped with some dope?" he says. "Fuck no," I answer. "They got me on assault cause Pat beat the crackhead ass, but the crackhead said me and Pat clicked on him."

"Somebody had called the police initially on me and Lil' Puss fighting," I continue. "But things had gotten twisted up when the law arrived. Me being 6'1½" with skin the color of polished leather boots, with two hundred and fifteen pounds of toned muscle from good genes, not good exercise or healthy eating. So I was already suspect," I finish.

"Infamous, I know I told you I wouldn't speak on this shit ever," Lil' 50 begins cautiously, "But you my nigga. You better leave Lil' Puss alone before you get fucked off for real," he advises. I nodded. I knew he was right.

"I already got a plan set," I inform. "My b-day comin' up and that's my b-day present to myself. But I gotta take care of Bo first," I say.

"What he do now?" 50 inquires, frustration showing in his face.

"He done told muthafuckas he ran me off the block. So I'm goin' straight there and checking all the spots 'til I catch up with him," I say deadpan. 50 was looking at me like I had lost my damn mind. Bo is what they call a bounty hunter. He has a set and I don't. But that didn't stop me any other time we bumped heads. "Man, don't look at me like that," I say to 50, still looking concerned. "If that shit spread, my respect gon' be flat-weeded."

"Yeah, I know infamous," Lil 50 agrees. He didn't look too happy about my plans though. "You know I got you bro, but I can't bring my set into this shit," he reminds.

"That's cool with me bro. I got to find Pat, too. We already said we was gone meet up," I say, changing the subject.

"Let's go then." 50 says, ready to move on.

Chapter 1

"Infamous, don't be comin' round here with that bullshit,"
my homegirl Racheal tells me as soon as she see me stroll up
on the block. "It's been quiet since you been gone!"
I guess she thinks I am showing up to shut some shit down.
The block starts where Elgin turns to Westheimer and goes
straight through to the southwest. It's so much money that
muthafuckers from all hoods come to the block at different
points to make money and don't bump heads.
"I ain't on nothing lil momma," I say assuring her.
"I'm just passing 'through. You seen Pat?"
"Yeah, he was over on Hyde and Park a while ago."
'That nigga know I don't fuck 'round back there' I say to
myself.
"Say lil momma you think you can tell him to meet you at
Cherry Park?" I asked.
No way was I going back there.
"I got you."
Bet that!"
Here I am out of the county all of 12 weeks and I'm already
in the midst of some crazy shit.
"Infamous!" I heard my name behind me.

"Damn Pat. You tryin' to work me tonight or something?" I asked, turning around seeing Pat.

He was brown skinned with an athletic build. He had on a graphic tee with heavy starched short black Nike cortex was pulled on over white ankle socks.

"Naw nigga, I just got through choppin' it up with this chick on Fairview" Pat responded.

"She got a homegirl!"

We smiled.

"Pat, you know damn well a nigga can't roam 'round there without some heat on his waist and some work in his drawers."

"Nigga have I fucked you yet?" He had me on that one. One thing about Pat: the nigga was paranoid as hell. So if he say it's, cool then you can bet your bottom dollar plus some.

"Aiight!" I said looking at the fool; "the homegirl better not look like that monkey off Congo either!"

"You'll still hit it nigga don't act new!"

"Only if she pay!" We both laughed cause that's how we do: we toss bitches and make them pay us. Sometimes we get two chicks ready for whatever. The problem occurs when it's two of them. Then we have to divide and conquer. Make them pay separately.

As we hit Fairview I spot this dark chocolate thick beauty she resembles a thick version of Ashley off the T.V show 'Fresh Prince of Bel Air'. She had on tight blue jeans and a white cut off top that looked printed on. Her breasts had to be about a 34DD.

"Pat!" I said stopping in my tracks.

"Yeah," he answers frowning at me.

"You see that fine ass black mare across the street?

"Where at?"

"Across the street at the corner nigga!" He follows my gaze and whistles.

"Damn bro, we might need to call a raincheck on them other hoes if we go after that!"

I don't know what he meant by that.

"Real spit, we in for a long night fucking with her." He said studying her. "You think we can break her down?

Infamous, I'll say this. Even if we can't get her to break it'll be worth the try!" Pat looked at me and smiled.

"You know what you might be on to something Pat" I said, looking at black beauty and loving what I see. It's like she can sense us with our radar on her because she turns and makes eye contact.

Fuck! Decision made! As we get closer I notice this chick has a face of a model with high cheekbones and the body of a video vixen.

"What's good shorty? Can you spare a minute?" I ask as I walk up on her.

"Depends," she says sassily.

"On what?" I reply.

"What your conversation's about. If it ain't up to standards, it's a waste of time and that costs coins!" She responds like a boss bith. I'm already diggin' this bitch secretly.

"I can dig that," I say, looking her over approvingly.

"I'm Infamous and this is my brother Pat," I say, introducing myself as I point out Pat.

"What's your name?" I ask.

"Everybody calls me Diva," she answers, giving me the once over.

"What you two doing out this time of night?" she asks.

"The hustle calls for the dollar and it can't be made sittin' on our ass!" Pat responds for the both of us.

"What's your hustle?" she asks, eager to see whether we an opportunity that interests her.

"Like Malcolm X its by any means necessary. You make a call and the "Get it Boys comin', ya feel me?" I reply.

"What's your profession and occupation short?" Pat cuts in. Diva looks from Pat to me as we hold contact for a minute. "I'm a boss bitch that, like ya'll, can get my paper more ways than one."

"Oh okay, I see where this is goin'" I say excitedly. But then somehow, I get this feeling like I know this chick from somewhere. I never forget a face so I start pondering the connection, studying her face and body language.

"I hope this conversation is headed toward a profit because I don't know any other language," she says beating me to the punch. Oh this is gonna be fun, I think to myself. I love Diva's feistiness.

"You want a profit to be topic?" I say, I got something for her.

"I'm a M.A.C., ya feel me? That's a man about cashflow. You got two Boss nigga's in your face that know the lingo." I let her know. I'm really starting to feel the vibes as I continue to speak.

"That's our talk." I add.

"I'm a T.O.P.S. type nigga" Pat chimes in.

That's the original pistol starter. So let's talk profit without loss. I like your style and I know Infamous does too." He shares, cutting his eyes at me.

"We sell dope, we jack, and we slang dick. The con is on point and the hustle we have is unique. We the Jack of all trades and the masters of many. Show us some money and we gone make a way to get it." Pat added slyly on some Dolemite type mannerisms. His body language, his tone, his stance, was on some ghetto poetic shit. He was on a roll.

"To show you we not slow, simple or stupid let me tell you your profession but not your occupation." Pat drills in.

"Your profession is as an escort to be politically correct." I take up the vibe from Pat. We got that chemistry. That's why we're the perfect team.

12

"You employer is the dollar bill. Now notice we speaking on your profession and not occupation, I'll let Pat lace you in on that one. Understand that? When we say 'by any means' that's exactly what we mean. You say you the same."

"Now let me cut you off for a minute", Diva cuts me off.

"I see you two think you ready for a bitch like me. I don't join teams. My team is *joined*. Infamous right?" She says looking at me.

"My profession ain't escort, it's money management" Diva declared.

As she kept talking, I kept studying her. This girl was familiar.

"I'll tell you what, answer this for me cause this shit keep buggin' me. What school you went to?" I asked.

"Middle or High?

"Both."

"I went to Welch MS"

I start to go back through my memory. Her face looks so familiar now.

"Niesha." I question remembering.

"Nigga how you know me?" She frowned now, studying my eyes.

"Well, Welch MS 1998 we had a class or two together, you sat in front."

I could see in her eyes that she's remembering.

"The only difference now is you filled out."

"Nigga I thought I knew you," her eyes light up with recognition. "You sat in the back always tappin', your fuckin pencil gettin' on my nerves. But now that that shit is out the way, let's talk money!" Diva said, getting back to the business!

Chapter 2

After meeting Diva and explaining shit to Pat, now I get to get rid of Lil Puss' destructive ass. I hear the shower going so I know Pat is up I look down at Lil Puss. She looks so beautiful and peaceful but as soon as she wakes up......

"Lil Puss" I whisper trying to wake her up gently.

"Hmmm?" she responds sleepily with her eyes still closed.

"Wake up momma we need to talk!"

I don't know if it was the tone I used or what. But whatever it was her eyes snapped open and I see the fire burning in her eyes. Good thing I had Pat move her shit.

"Talk about what?" She asked, becoming fully awake.

She sat up in the bed wearing only panties no bra. I hear the shower cut off Pat's finished. Good.

"About us and what we doing to each other!"

"What's that supposed to mean?" She asked, scowling. Lil Puss is small. She's like a super Ghetto Jada Pinkett Smith. Her light brown eyes got a Chinese like slant. She's small but she's a tornado when provoked. I know shit's coming next. I really don't want to deal with her right now. But I need to. I'm trying to gather my emotions, choose my words carefully.

"Nigga, what's that supposed to mean?"

"Lil Puss you know I love you," I begin calmly. "But shit ain't right with us."

I look her in her eyes. "When shit fucked up you go from me to Bo. Then you want to leave when shit don't go your way. I just got out of jail because of some bullshit with us." She looks me in the eye.

"Nigga, we gone talk this out and we gone be good!" she responds. Wrong answer!

"Naw Lil Puss we're done, we got to end this chapter lil momma!"

Pat comes out of the bathroom and we lock eyes. He goes straight for the door. Coward!!

"You got me fucked up nigga!" Lil Puss yelled jumping out of the bed. Aww shit!

"You ain't goin' nowhere. We gonna talk 'bout this shit!"

I get out the bed and began putting my clothes on before she can snatch them up.

"Answer this. How'd I lose my job?"

"That was not my fault!" she defends.

"The fuck it wasn't!" Now I'm getting angry. I got a weed and assault charge because this bitch wanted to fight and act a donkey.

"I told them you did not touch me," she defends again.

"I don't matter what you told them. The shit could've been avoided. I'm steady taking losses fucking with you. How can a nigga make money and keep money if we losing money 'cause a nigga getting locked up!" I said; ready to be done with Lil Puss and her bullshit-ass dramatic water works.

Just then Pat walks through the door. When he nods and goes back out the door I hit her with the bomb.

"I want to be with somebody else!" I watch her closely while I speak.

"She 'bout her paper and she ain't with the drama. So you

16

can go find Bo or I can go find him for you!" Finished dressing, I turn to leave.

Wham! Where the floor come from?

"Oh you big dicking now?" Lil Puss, standing over me talking shit.

Ain't this a bitch. This bitch done put her hands on me again.

"You just gonna try to drop me like I'm a nothing ass bitch" she raves.

I pick myself off the floor, my head hurting.

"See that's what makes you nothing" I say angrily, rubbing my head." A nothin' ass broke down bitch would have helped me find the fucking door!!"

I walked out the door but not before I hear her scream out.

"Fuck you bitch ass nigga!!"

I still can see her in my mind standing there topless talking shit to a closed door cause I'm gone!

"That went well!" Pat joked. It would have been funny if my head wasn't aching from where she popped a nigga.

"Let's go before she realize I left her with what I met her with," I say to Pat while walking away.

"Good idea!" Pat says following me.

"You know you bleeding like a stuck pig, bro!" Pat informs me.

"No shit where?" I start looking down at the robin egg blue Polo shirt I had put on.

"Straight head shot! Look at the shirt!"

That's impossible because she hit me in the back of my head "Bitch!" I cursed. This bitch done drew blood.

"That she is bro. You want me to call Diva?"

"Naw bro. she don't need to see a nigga like this!" I shook my head.

"After all the game we done spit, let that shit marinate for a few days. If we see her or run into her then we'll go from

17

there!"

"So what you wanna do? Sittin' on our ass ain't no option," Pat stated wisely. "We goin' to the block or are we going to the west?"

"Da west been calling my name for a couple of weeks now. It's time to put our uniforms on and go to work. We can re-up when we run into Diva cause something tells me we gone need some bread!!"

...

"What time is it?" Pat asks.

"10:05!" I answer. It's dark out and we been laying in wait for something to sting.

"We been ducked off for 2 good minutes bro. I think we need to change spots!" Pat said, anxious for some action.

"Give it a minute or two. It's been too quiet," I responded, trying to calm Pat down.

Patience is a virtue, but I can understand Pat's anxiousness and impatience. Usually you could count on Woodfair to produce a good lick in no time flat. But tonight was a slow night for the hoes and the johns, and we had been hidden out for about ½ an hour. Traffic was slow tonight.

We had been sitting in the parking lot of the "Villa de Cancun" apartments patiently waiting for some action. The game Gods must have heard my prayer. Because just then a little black Ford Focus pulls in.

"Check it out" I said needlessly, "It's two heads in that ride?"

"Looks like a female in the passenger seat!"

Bingo!

"You know the routine; circle and get in position." I said coaching. "When I see her head go down and his head go back, I'm coming full speed!"

"Infamous, what about the hoe?" Pat asks.

"What about her? You know the target is the trick!" I glance

18

at him making sure everything is still understood.

"Okay," Pat nods his head. "Catch and finish him quick!"

"If the hoe scream, snatch the trick out and close the door!"

"I'm gone!" like a ghost he disappears into the dark.

I keep my eyes on the car. Before Pat gets to his spot the hoe head leaves sight. A few seconds later the dude head falls back. I take off like a rocket. As I reach the car Pat appears out of nowhere right next to me. I snatch the door open and Pat snatches the trick. The lanky black man comes out headfirst with his plants at his ankles. With practiced ease Pat puts the man to sleep while I'm rifling through the man's pockets. I hear Pat curse.

"Ain't this a bitch! Look who's in the car?" I follow Pat's eyes and I'll be damned.

"Diva?" I question frowning. "I'll be damned, just when I thought this was gonna be a boring night!"

"Finish yo job, we can talk later."

Diva putting Pat's focus back on the business at hand.

"Pat strip him," I say, getting in position to apply pressure to the trick's neck, because he starts to come around.

"Goodnight Prince charming!" I say as I put him back out. After he's stripped we throw the clothes into the car. I look and Diva's already in the driver's seat.

"Where to?" she asks, pulling out of the spot where the car was parked.

"Hit the creek and make a left," I instruct. I look around and make sure no one is watching us or witnessed our caper.

"It's another set of apartments that's half empty we can go through the car in!"

We find the apartments and park. We start to go through the car like we're the law and they got hidden compartments of dope and money.

"Diva you got your car out here?" I ask.

"It's on Lansdale at the Premier."

"We gonna take you to your car and Pat gone ride with you," I start to lay out the plan to them. "We going to Sandpiper to Regency Square to drop this bitch off until we can get rid of it!"

"I know where that is," Diva states.

"Well I know the back streets so try to keep up or you'll get lost. I'm for real!" I inform her.

"Bet I get there before you!" She says giving me a look.

"Don't lose no money lil' momma. This my neck of the woods!" I warn.

"$20 bet?" She asks

"Don't do it!" Pat warns. "He really know what he's doing."

"Bet or not?" She asks, determined to lose her money.

"Bet!" I say confidently. I give Pat a smirk.

As we get to her car, her and Pat jumps out once I park. Her car is a white Galant and looks like it can push. I'm in a Ford Focus. I watch her get into her car. Allow her to start up. And we're off!

We make the left on Bissonnet and drive like bats out of hell. Instead of taking the turn off Braeswood, I go down Bissonnet until I pass the golf course. I make the right and I see Diva brake fast. I slow down until I see her headlights behind me.

'This gone be the easiest $20 I've ever made!' I say to myself as we come to Fondren she takes the lead and makes a left on Braeswood. But I keep straight. When I reach Willow Bend I make the left so I can come from behind the apartments. When I make the left on Sandpiper and head to the entrance I see a set of head lights coming towards me so I stop at the gate an lower my window. I hear Lil Wayne's "Hustler's Musik" banging in her trunk as Diva pulls up behind me. I lead her to the back of the apartments.

As I get out I look around at the Lexus in the lot that Pat and me jacked a week ago. The only reason it was still parked

20

there was because the shop we usually dealt with was afraid that the car had a GPS tracker on it.

"So what y'all call this?" Dive asks getting out of her car, looking around.

 "Da Lot ," Pat answers.

"How you come up on this?" She inquires.

"My cousin use to stay in the apartment right there." I point up at an upstairs apartment.

The apartment was surrounded by other vacant apartments. "He left me the key and lightbulb's lit up for me."

"So all the cars y'all hit for comes here?" Damn this bitch asks a lot of questions.

"Naw, some get cleaned out and left on the side of the road while others are sold for parts."

"Sometimes we use them until we run out of gas," Pat added.

"Y'all two niggas move quick. Y'all work; cleanin' that shit took all of 10 seconds from start to finish. Then 5 to 10 minutes to get here," she said approvingly. "I can tell y'all are professional!"

"Not really!" says Pat.

"Y'all do this a lot?" she asked me. What's up with this bitch and all this 21 question shit!

"Not really we only go this route when our backs are against the wall and we got a goal set and a mission to accomplish!" Pat answers.

"So how much y'all get from this lick?"

"We don't count until our shift is over," I respond, looking at her funny.

"When we get tired!!" Pat and me say in unison.

"Are you tired yet?" she asks, looking at both of us.

"Not by a long shot!"

"That's for fucking sure!"

Chapter 3

1 month later.

"Where the fuck you nigga's been hiding? We ain't heard a peep out of you two niggas!"

My big homey PX say, letting Pat and me into his sparsely furnished house. He's wearing jogging pants and a tank top. He looks like a young college athlete. His light brown skin baby smooth.

"Money's been the motive!" I answer, giving him dap and moving into his house followed by Pat.

"Yeah I dig that. But you niggas been M.I.A. for a hot minute!" Lil 50 states, sitting on the leather couch smoking a sweet.

"We ain't the ones with all the time in the world to fuck off," Pat says, looking around the house. "Shit last time I seen you that blue Blazer was bumping and dope was falling out the tailpipe!"

"Shit last time I seen Lil 50 we had just got out the country," I said looking at Lil 50 wearing a brand new everything.

"Right point made, what's good, what up?" 50 asks.

"We need some heat,' I say.

"Problems?" 50 asks, looking me in the eyes.

"Naw, hustle!" Pat informs him.

"What you looking for? Something big or small?" PA asks.
"Not too big or small, but two of 'em" I say, not caring
exactly what we get, just needing tools for the hustle.
"It'll be a couple of days."
"Shit nigga we need them in a couple of hours!" Pat says.
"Let me make some calls. Y'all don't need no dope?"
"Naw!" We was good on that end. Ever since Pat and I
hooked up with Diva we found out her brother was on, and
we was getting love. "Just the heat," Pat said.
"You two are up to something and keeping quiet. Infamous
I understand but Pat you're extra tight lipped," 50 says,
observing us closely.
"I know, right? What's really good?" PA agrees.
"We told y'all, money is the motive and profit is the topic,"
Pat states. "We just grindin' hard!"
"I know what that means for you two niggas," PA says,
smiling at the both of us.
"I'm surprised whatever lock y'all hittin ain't burning up."
He's fishing for information. Trying to get us to tell him
what we been on.
"Straight up!" 50 adds. "Last time y'all went on a run,
Fairview, Hyde Park, and Westheimer was smoking like a
California wildfire. "
"Damn, it wasn't that bad!" Pat defended.
"The fuck it wasn't. Niggas couldn't even walk around
without getting pulled over and searched down!!" PA
argued.
"Ain't you supposed to be making some phone calls ole
mark ass nigga? I remind him.
"The truth burns!" he says laughing before he gets up and
exits the room.
"All bullshit to the side, you nigga's good?" 50 asks
seriously.
"Yeah a little better than usual!" I answer.
24

Just then 50's phone spits out Webbie's "Bad Bitch." I know the ringtone 'cause we share the same.

"Hella," he answers. "Aight, sure? Bet." I follow the one-sided conversation. He hangs up the phone and looks at me. I look at Pat.

"Call Diva and tell her it's gone have to be a drive-by to pick us up and we gone have to change in the car."

Before Pat can call, "Bad Bitch" By Webbie sings from my phone.

"Sexy Black, talk to me!" I answer.

"Tell me something good and I'll tell you something better!" Diva. It sounds like an angle. But I know she's more lethal than a hollow point dipped in acid.

"I ain't got nothing good right now. But the news is we got what we went for," I respond. "Other than that we pushin on time. It's gone have to be a grab and go for us and a drive by for you. We gone have to change in the car."

"Thanks for the heads up. Something told me to grab the girls first," she said.

"You ain't got to rush, just get to Da Lot ASAP. We'll be there in 10-15 minutes."

"Cool, 'cause we already here!" Who? Ain't that a bitch. I hang up.

"Well Pat, she was 3 steps ahead on this one," I relay to Pat. "She already there with the chicks and waiting on us!"

"Time for some music," Pat says, turning on Tupac's 'Me and my Girlfriend."

As we exit interstate 59 at Bissonnet we pull up to the light. I turn my head checking the mirrors. A familiar car pulls up beside us. When I recognize who it is, I elbow Pat. He looks, and changes the disc to Ludacris's "Hoe." We sing along loudly with the song catching Puss attention. We both gives her the finger. I pull off into the turn and we go about our business.

"You see that hoe face." I ask Pat remembering the screw face she gave us.

"Wait and see how that hoe look when she sees us with Diva," Pat says laughing.

15 minutes later we pulling into Da Lot We notice two bad ass yellows who damn near look like twins. They both stand about 5'5", cute face, slim waist, and big behind. Damn! Standing next to them is that sexy black chocolate that a nigga been fiending for.

I never been one for dark broads but Diva give the other two a run for they money and collects first place.

"Damn, they did say the #1 way to set a nigga up is with pussy he can't resist!!!" I say out loud as we get out the car and approach Diva and her girls.

"Be lucky we on the same team." Diva says to us.

"We all lucky we on the same team!!" Pat corrects.

"Point taken," Diva responds. An awkward moment of silence ensues.

"Okay we can shoot the shit later. What's the situation?" I ask, breaking the tension.

"It's a two-part deal?" Diva starts. "First we hit the stroll hard as fuck and then we move to the set up!"

"And they are?" I ask, directing attention to the two yellow broads.

"Capable and willing to make this paper and go about they way," Diva responds, sounding like a female mack.

"At least we know this a temporary get together with them," Pat cuts in. "Even though I'd love to get to know them a whole lot better."

"Whatever," Diva says, sucking her teeth. "Are y'all gone get ready, or drool over these hoes?!"

Checkmate.

Chapter 4

"Infamous, let me set the mood on this one," Pat tells me sounding crazy.

"Nigga remember this ain't no petty bullshit we gone head to County on!" I warn him.

"Bruh, cut the shit!" Pat responds letting me know he's on point.

"Aight!"

"I wish you two niggas would get y'all heads out yo ass!" Diva says bringing the focus back to the business at hand. It takes Pat a full 5 minutes to give us the rundown on the plan that's going through his head. I got to admit it's fire.

"So all I need to do is be at the back window?" I ask making sure I'm getting everything.

"You know the motto," Pat says. "Quiet robberies or loud homicides!"

"Diva, you sure ain't no dogs in the backyard?" I ask. We don't need no surprises.

"If I jump back there and get hit, I'm gone come back and bite your ass after I shoot the damn dog!"

"Nigga I been setting this up for a while I just need a few more pieces to the puzzle," she assures me. "Unless he bought a dog last night, it's only 3 niggas inside."

"Aight, I'm down!"

...

When we arrive at the location I get out the car putting on gloves. I head to the house that's next to our target house. The house we're about to hit got lights on and the front door is wide open. I make my way to the back of the appropriate house.

"Quarter horse nigga. That's twenty-five in ebonics!" I hear as I'm headed to the back of the house. Now I know at least two of the niggas are playing dominoes. I keep moving around back and jump the fence. I got the two up front playing dominoes.

So where is the third nigga at? I hear the knock at the front door and at the same time the phone vibrates in my pocket. The text tells me that the third dude came out the bathroom. It feels like I been waiting for hours. But in reality all I been waiting is just a couple of minutes. I'm looking around the backyard waiting on my cue and spot this barbeque spit that looks like it came out the showroom.

'Yeah its money in this bitch,' I think to myself. All of a sudden everything goes quiet. It's like even the small critters and crickets stop all movements and sound. I hear the window above my head open. I listen intently for my cue. Chris Brown's "Poppin" comes on and I'm on my feet. Quickly I climb through the window and head to the the bathroom door with gun in hand. I hear the girls giggling and smacking skin.

I stop and text Pat: *You ready?*

Immediately he reply: *at the door!*

I ease up the hallway towards the sound of the music. I can see the front door from where I'm at. So I wait for my last cue. As the song ends Diva walks to the door and looks out. She unlocks the screen. As she moves away T.Pain's "I'm In Love With A Stripper" blasts from the speakers somewhere in the house.

I watch Pat walk through the front door and I put the pistol to the first muthafucker I see.

"If y'all don't know what this is I'll be happy to explain!" Pat says.

Closing the door behind him I make a point by hitting the guy I got at gunpoint in the head with the pistol.

"Aaahh! What's that for?" the guy screams. Pussy!

"My explanation!"

"Ladies strip theses niggas down to they tighty whities" Pat says directing.

"You got the duct tape?" I ask him.

"Yeah," he answers, producing what's gonna restrain these guys so we can

do what we do. As each dude gets stripped I duct tape mouths, wrists and ankles.

"Tear this bitch up and grab everything worth something." I tell everybody. "We gone empty this bitch like we leaving the state."

"Unless these fuck boys got something we can take and get the fuck out right now." Pat said, looking at the 3 dudes duct taped. "Anybody want to help?"

"Ain't you glad we brought the U-haul?" I lie, trying to get one of them to give up something useful.

"Yeah, it's gone make this shit look easy!" Pat says, catching on quickly.

That's why I fuck with this nigga! Just then one of the niggas go buck wild. He's young, slim, not really built for no gangsta shit, you can see the softness in his eyes. Whom! I hit him with the pistol. The weakest link.

"Quiet yo bitch ass down unless you got some information! Do you?" He nods his head. Bingo! Pat takes the duct tape from his mouth.

"Okay, you get a chance. Money, dope, and jewelry. Where

is it??"

"The dope is in the kitchen." He immediately started
spilling the beans. "Ain't no money 'cause we used it on the
re-up and we don't rock no jewelry." So he wants to lie too.
"I'll check the kitchen but they lying about the money and
jewelry bro," Pat said, telling me what I already knew.
'I know!" Pat goes right to the kitchen and goes to tearing it
up. Hearing all the mass destruction going on, big dude
goes to squirming and trying to speak. I go and take the
tape from his mouth.

"C'mon man.There's a cabinet under the sink with a
falsewall." he whines.

"Pat! Under the sink there's a false wall!" I yell out.

"I'm on it!"

"What about us?" Diva asks. They were all fully dressed,
having taken care of their end of the caper.

"Hold that thought!" I tell Diva, holding up a finger.

"I know you lying about the money and jewels," I tell the
big dude. "I'm gone give you one more chance against my
better judgment. So forget the jewelry; where the money
at?" I ask, looking at him intently.

"Now before you answer we know that we gone tear this
bitch up anyway until we find what we know is here. So
think real hard before you speak," I warn.

The two other guys are real quiet and not moving so I know
it's some slick shit in the mix.

"Come here," I motion Diva over.

"Check this bitch for guns. The sofas, all the cushions. The
beds, under the mattresses. The closets and every nook and
cranny in the bathroom!"

I tell her we ain't missing nothing if I can help it.

"You two help her," I tell the other two chicks.

When they leave its just me and the three dummies.

"Now let's get serious!" I say.

30

Chapter 5

"Damn nigga!" Diva said with admiration coloring her voice. "I don't know what you did or said but it worked fast as fuck!"

"I know what he said and did," Pat said, looking at me knowingly

"Damn nigga! You gone give up the game!?!" I respond looking at Pat accusingly. This nigga might, trying to impress the two yellow broads and Diva.

"Not unless the pay is good," Pat says jokingly.

"Fuck it, I might as well tell it," I say, beating Pat to the punch.

"Look, I keep a knife on me at all times. Niggas are scared of death. But when you tell them what you gone do to them and how you gone do it the imagination takes over and goes wild."

"So what did you say?" one of the girls asks.

"Shit basically that I'm gone cut their dick off, watch them scream out and bleed out," I answer. "While they imagine that, I take my knife out so they can see it. I tell them that I'm gone cut their assholes out. Then its ashes to ashes and dust to dust!"

"Ashes to ashes dust to dust, what that mean?" Diva asks. Here she go with all these damn questions.

"Okay, who the fuck are you and what you do?" This nigga trippin.

"I'm the same nigga that was there when you first did that shit" Pat responds, missing the point of my sarcasm. "I didn't know if you were serious or playing."

"Who said I wasn't serious if I didn't believe that they told the truth?"

Silence took over. I remember what he was talking about. That day when we ran through a garage on some false information. I let the threat out about their kids and still couldn't find shit. So we left them duct taped and the kids were untied so they could get them loose after we left.

"Know what, moving on," Diva said, getting the picture. "The next lick is different."

"How's that?" I asked.

"He's an old client of mine," Diva began to explain. "So it has to look like y'all just popped up. I got a plan for all that and y'all can tweak it so it works for y'all."

"Can I make a guess at your plan?" I ask.

"Go ahead."

"Don't do it Infamous!" Pat cut, warning me.

"No I want to hear this," Diva says, challenging me. "I'm all ears."

"You want it to look random. So you either gone meet him at a hotel or you gone have him pick you up."

I look at her to see if I'm getting it right so far.

"Keep going," Diva says, listening.

"That's when the problem comes in." I say, poking holes in the foolproof plan she thought she had. "If we get him as he meet you or pick you up he'll know it's a set up. So your plan got to both take care of the problem and have the solution!"

"Exactly. Two birds with one stone," she says." But we can say fuck it and I'll never see him in this life or the next."
I knew then that she was a total gangsta. My type of woman.
"So where we headed?" I ask. "Just fasten your seatbelt and enjoy the ride for a while!"
"Does anybody understand exactly what's being said right here?" Pat directs his question to the two yellows. "This might be a highway to hell." Pat sometimes just needs to shut the fuck up. But this is my nigga though.
"Shit, I'm down." Diva speaks. "As long as the positions are covered I have no worries about no bullshit." Diva is a thoroughbred.
"What are you looking at me for, Pat?" I ask, frowning at that nigga. "You know that business is always a plus!!"
"Everybody needs to hear it. They don't know you like I do dumbass!" Pat said. "I know this nigga ain't clowning."
"Yeah I need to know what's up," Diva states. "I'm down for the crown. A day one veteran in this shit."
"Let's get this money!" I state.
"I have a question though," Pat says. "What about these two back here?"
I look into the mirror at the two females in the back; almost forgot about them.
"Earlier we said they were here for just a moment." Pat shook his head." I still don't know their names."
"Me either. Ain't this a bitch we slipping."
"I meant what I said. Now if they minds have changed they can speak for themselves," Diva says.
"I'm Champagne," says one with an accent I can't catch. She has a long straight black weave. I notice she have pretty light green eyes. "I'm 'bout that dollar. This is Red," she says, introducing the other chick. Red's eyes are dark, probably a dark brown. "I speak for her."

Well!!

Silence envelopes the car for a minute.

"Well I definitely didn't see that coming," Pat says catching my eyes in the rear-view mirror.

"Good enough for me," Diva says. Already she knew the deal with the two.

"What's so special about Red?" I add my 2 cents.

"I'm spoken for," Red answers up in a voice that sounds like she smoke about two packs of Newports a day.

"She's a live one," Pat says smiling. "I like her."

"I guess we're all spoken for now," Diva puts in.

...

"Who gone count the money?" Pat asks. We're driving back from the lick and now it's time to start passing out duty slips. We have to divide up the chores. "I'm fucking with the burners!" Pat assigned himself a job.

"I can fuck with the dope." Diva volunteers. "My brother and I know how to handle dope!"

"If that's the case I got the dope and you manage the money, since that's your profession," I say.

"So I guess we got the jewelry," Champagne announces from her position in the back. "Pawn or street sell?" she asks. I like Champagne.

"Just get rid of it for the most that you can," Pat says.

"Do we do the split now, or after everything is over?" I ask so it could be understood by everybody.

"We can do it now at least so everyone will know what's in the pot. We need to know our beginning worth," Diva states.

I don't know what all that means. But whatever.

"That's a bet! Diva count the money when we get to the spot. I'm gonna figure out how much the dope is worth," I say figuring everything out. "Pat, keep us the best burners for now we gone stash the rest until we need them!"

"What about the other lick? We still got the problem!" Pat reminds us

"No we don't," Diva says laying that to rest. "I been texting since we been talking."

Damn I think I love this bitch; she's always on top of her shit.

"So it's a go?" I ask

"Of course."

"When we gone get there?" I ask, ready for the next J.O.B.

"We need to switch cars" Diva says, "so I think we should go by Da Lot and grab the truck!"

"Where we gone meet him at?" Pat asks.

"The Astro Inn on South Main. That way we got 2 or 3 exits from the area!" Diva stated wisely.

Yeah. This bitch is a keeper for real.

"How much duct tape we got left?" I ask. We need to stay ready to keep from getting antsy.

"Enough!" Pat says.

"We must be the bait?!" Champagne states the obvious.

"Actually, we all gone be in the room," Diva tells her.

"Infamous and Pat is gonna be in the bathroom. As soon as the door closes it's a wrap like Reynolds!!"

"Do you know how much he's bringing with him?" I ask Diva.

"No but he gone have cash and credit card. All we need to do is get him to give us the pin number for cards. One of us can handle that while the rest stay with him in the room with pressure on him," she answers.

"Let's get this money," Pat says "I'll even go with the cards so we ain't got to talk about that no more!"

"I second that motion. Matter of fact are we there yet?" I said.

"Nigga, you stupid," said Red. Wow. The bitch ain't scared to talk

"No, I'm bored," I state.

"Fire this up!" Diva said reaching inside her bra and pulling a sweet of that dynamic."Sit back we're almost there!"

"If he fire that up he might shut up!" Pat says. The nigga is turning into a regular comedian all of a sudden.

"How about fuck both of y'all," I say "Cue the music up 'til we get to Da Lot "

Pat puts in "The Carter 3" and we listen as Lil Wayne does his best shit. I spark the blunt up and I look around at everybody in the car. Diva's in the driver's seat and Pat sits next to her in the passenger seat. I'm back in the back beside Champagne and Red. Everything we just hit for is in the trunk next to the 15's that's banging hard.

"Pat," I say.

"Infamous."

"We got a problem!"

"And that is ?"

"We can't have all our shit in the spot with us " I say thinking about what would happen if we got pulled over or anything. "We need a stash spot."

"We can use Da Lot ," Pat says.

"I thought about that but I'm the only one with a key," I say. "It's gone be times visits are gonna need to be made by each of us."

"You know I ain't got no problem with it but I see your point." Pat says. "We really need a spot."

"It can be the vault for a minute," Diva said. "Shit, with the lick we just hit and the one we're about to hit we'll be straight!"

"I hope so," I say really ready to hit a big lick so I could chill for a minute. Relax and enjoy life. As we pull into Da Lot I notice an extra car next to the Explorer.

"Company!" Pat said, noticing the same thing I did at the same time.

36

"I see em!"

I never seen the car before so my antennas are up and I'm on high alert. I pull the pistol from my waist band and place it on my lap. A car on the Lot is only supposed to be put there by

me or Pat.

"That's for me!" Diva says, drawing a scowl from me. Is this bitch serious? "What's up with you two?"

Dumb question from Diva. She just dropped a couple of notches in my eyes.

"One we don't know the car, and two it isn't supposed to be here," Pat says, noticing two people sitting in the car.

"That's my boyfriend!" Diva says trying to calm everything down.

This bitch has to be crazy!

"Can I shoot em?" Pat asks.

"Only if I can too!" I add.

"That's my boyfriend," Diva states again. No shit! I guess she don't think we heard her the first time.

"He's trespassing. This is private property," I say, feeling evil.

'It's apartments!" Red said, speaking up when she's supposed to be shutting up.

"Possession is nine tenths of the law." Pat says. His voice low and sinister.

"You two are crazy!" Champagne says. Another one speaking up when she's supposed to be shutting up.

"No, we're serious!" I say, ready to pop off.

"Dead ass!" Pat adds.

"Get rid of him," Pat tells Diva.

"We need a new spot." I say not feeling Diva's boyfriend knowing where we lay our game down. Diva gets out of the car and heads to the white Chevy.

"I still say we should shoot him."

"Cut it out!" Champagne cuts in. Whatever happened to the quiet Champagne? I like that one better. "You probably mad cause you thought she was single."

Yeah, I Prefer the quiet Champagne! The more I look towards Diva's boyfriend's car the stronger my feelings get. "I still say we shoot 'em!"

"Real spit," Pat agrees. "I say the same."

Chapter 6

"Pat and Infamous. This is Payne." Diva introduces us to her boyfriend. He's about 5'9" with a dirty red skin tone, his hair is long and in braids. He looks like a heavy version of Allen Iverson. I don't know what gave her the idea we wanted to meet this nigga.

"I hope he ain't a Payne in the ass," I mumble not really giving a damn if he heard me or not.

"Second that." Somebody heard me. Me and Pat made eye contact.

"Champagne's over there, we don't need another 'Payne'," I say, not really joking.

"I see where this is headed," Diva said, realizing she made a big ass mistake. "Look that's my bad for telling him to come to Da Lot. But I had to holla at him face to face about something." She apologized.

"Infamous, hold up a second," Pat says.

"For what?"

"We got to unload this issue and move around. What about him?" Pat said rolling his shoulders." Diva already knows the spot so you know she gone tell him."

Pat pointing out the obvious.

"Look homey," Payne cut us off." I'm just here for my baby. Whatever y'all set up here is it ain't my business."

"I say we shoot him and get it over with," I say, masking the plan.

"Why you keep wanting to shoot somebody. You need to stop that shit." Diva said with a slight attitude. Ain't this a bitch! Just when you want to believe Diva is a veteran bitch, she start doing rookie shit.

"Where we gone put the body?" Pat asks, ignoring Diva and her attitude.

"In the trunk and drop his body off in the bayou on the way to the next lick," I answer.

We talkin' about this nigga like he already dead and not standing in front of us.

"Y'all still on the dumb shit or are we gone go get this money or what?" Champagne, man this bitch got this annoying ass habit of speaking at the wrong time. "I didn't sign up for no crazy we can't profit from!"

"Thank you," Diva said, opening her big ass mouth.

"Don't thank me 'cause they only doing this 'cause they like you!"

Me and Pat exchange glances and frown. How dare this bitch!

"Red, come get you speaker before she enter the Fuck You zone with nigga boy," I say, tired of Champagne's mouth.

"You ain't gone fuck with a picture of her," Red responds, coming up to where we all are standing.

"Infamous lets unload this shit," Pat says, putting our mind back on the business at hand.

"Can I just shoot everybody!" I say, turning to take care of the business.

"Only if we can shoot back," Red adds. Ha ha, very funny. While me and Pat unload the trunk, it looks like the conversation between Payne and

40

Diva is getting heated. I tap Pat as we stop and look over at Diva and her boyfriend.

"You seeing this?"

"Yeah. How much you want to bet we not the problem?" Pat ask, seeing something I didn't.

"Damn nigga hurt a nigga ego Powyaww!" I say, getting it now.

"You remember that chick Yolanda?" Pat asks.

"Yeah yeah. What about her?"

"She got a home girl that got that paper. She stay off 45 somewhere. That's all I know. but I need to find out." Pat says. But I don't know what the fuck that got to do with anything right now!

"What, do we need to go to Fairview?" I ask trying to see where he going with this conversation.

"Maybe if I can't catch Yolanda!" Pat answers.

"What, you two over here plotting our next lick?" Champagne asks, walking up on me and Pat where we had stopped behind the Explorer.

"*Our* next lick," Pat answers. It's good he answered because I wasn't about her scratch.

"It's not that type of lick. It's more sexual than violent on this one." Pat answered, cooling her heels.

"You serious?" She asks, studying Pat's face.

"You didn't get the speech did you?!" Pat glances at me then back to Champagne.

"We all around hustle's momma. If it's a dollar to be made and we can make it, it's got."

"Most niggas wouldn't do that!" Red says walking up joining the conversation.

"We ain't most niggas!" I remind.

"We can see that. I can see why y'all get along so good," Red observes.

"They think mostly alike too!" Champagne adds. It just

might be some hype for this bitch, I think.

"Don't say that cause then Pat gone think he smart." I smile at Pat.

"I'm not gonna even entertain that right now," Pat shoots back. "I'm watching Diva throw aggravated gang signs in Payne's face," he say, sending our attention over to Diva and her

boyfriend. Diva's fingers and hand look like they got a life of their own. Diva looks pissed to the highest level of piss-tivity, we finish putting our stash up. As we put the last bag in place we hear a car start and burn out. Looking around I see that Payne's car is gone.

"Where's Diva?" I ask.

"In her car." Champagne points.

"What you think Infamous?" Pat asks me.

"I think we should have shot him!" I'm back to that.

"Yeah," Pat agrees. That's why that's my nigga!

"You niggas something else!" Champagne says walking in the direction of Diva and her car. After I lock up the spot, I head to the truck; Diva steps out of her car with a blunt between her lips.

Pat taps me on the shoulder and says.

"Let her make it!"

"I ain't gone do nothing!" I respond defensively. This nigga knows me too well.

"Y'all ready?" Diva asks, walking up on us like nothing had just happened between her and boyfriend.

Let her make it Infamous. I hear Pat's voice in my mind.

"Yeah, we good to go!" Pat answers.

"I'll drive!" Diva volunteers

Let her make it Infamous.

"What's up on you and nigga-boy?" I couldn't help myself.

"Infamous!" Pat growls.

"It's not a problem!" Diva says.

42

"You sure?" I ask, studying her eyes.

"Infamous!" Pat growls again. Fuck Pat!

"Yeah I'm sure. Now are we gone get this money or are you gone worry about my love life?" Diva responds defensively.

"I can multi-task." I say. "What about you?"

"Man, if y'all gone shoot the shit let's do it on the way to the money," Pat said irritated.

"I call shot gun," I say.

"Is he always like this?" Champagne asks.

Does this broad ever know when to just shut the fuck up!

"This is him letting her make it!" Pat says.

"If that's letting her make it, I hate to see him try to piss her off," Red adds.

"He pisses me off, then he gone be asking me to let him make it," Diva says.

What the fuck.

"Y'all talk like I ain't even here," I say getting into the truck.

"It's called a warning before destruction," Diva says looking over at me. Really!

"It's called you got me bent," I respond.

"No its called Infamous getting duct taped if he keep on bullshitting around!" Pat spits, losing patience.

Rick Ross's "Hustlin'" comes on before I can answer. It might have saved me cause Pat sounded like he was ready to flip when he started talking about duct tape. One thing I'm not and that's a "Damn fool." True enough me and Pat been down since day one and we won't come to blows, I know how far to go with him. Diva cuts the music off.

"I got a confession to make," She starts. "I did that on purpose with Payne."

I frown, now this bitch didn't!

"I been finding shit out and I wanted him to see that I can move on if I need to and still make my bread."

43

This bitch has to be crazy. Blow our spot up just to prove a point to this bubble gum ass nigga.

"I fucked up bringing him to Da Lot ," she admits. Yeah, she sure did fuck up. "But I wanted him to see us all together!!" Wrong move!

"Infamous?" A silent question from Pat.

"You should have shot him!" Pat says, and I agree.

"We said that earlier. Champagne and Red sided with Diva on that one," I state.

"Y'all was serious?" Diva asks. Duh!

"We don't like complications," I start. "Him being there and seeing two niggas get out of your car and one was next to you. That's a complication!" I look over at Diva. Will I regret this union? At first things looked so promising. Now it's starting to look like this bitch can't think.

"What if I tell you, you two wasn't the problem?"

"I'll say it don't matter cause now he know 'bout Da Lot and the spot, and we don't know shit about him," Pat said. I could sense the anger coming off of Pat.

"I told you we should have shot him!" I add.

Chapter 7

Knock, knock. Me and Pat hear the door from the bathroom of the hotel room. Game time!

"Hold on!" Diva shouts.

"Damn girl!" We hear after a couple of moments of silence.

"What you wearing for me today? And who are these lovely ladies?"

We hear the voice of a white man.

"I thought I'd do something special today since you show me so much love." I hear Diva respond.

"Hell yeah! That's what I'm talking about"

"Let's take these clothes off baby" I hear Diva sweet talking. She's in her element.

"You ready?" Pat turns to me and asks. There's no response needed. Because my eyes and body language is answer enough.

"I can tell you ready for us!" The signal comes.

Before the guy knows what's going on he has two pistols in his face.

"You so much as breathe wrong your next sight gone be Jesus at the pearly gates asking to be let into heaven." I say to him meanly. He looked into my eyes and saw the coldness. So many emotions played across his face at once.

"Duct tape him," Pat says from behind me

"Don't move baby.It'll be easier!" Diva says soothingly. The guy gives a start and he looks at Diva wild eyed; so many emotions again cross his face.

"After all I've done for you, you do me like this!" He sound so hurt and miserable. Everybody know hoes can't be trusted. Damn fool he was!.

"Don't piss me off!" Diva says coldly, gave the guy a look that made him dry swallow and look away. Coward!

"Okay we can do this the easy way or the hard way," Pat says bringing the man's attention back to him.

"Your choice you give us the pin codes to all your cards, and they better be right. If you give us the run around, then you gone get fucked off!" I threatened.

Diva grabs the man's wallet and phone. She hands the credit cards to Pat. The driver's license to me and the phone to Champagne and Red, she holds the wallet and takes out all the cash.

"$423 dollars!" Diva counts frowning. "Muthafucka you came short today didn't you?"

Diva looked at the sweaty, pathetic looking trick.

"What's your going rate?" I ask Diva, just curious.

"$600"

"That better be some good 'pussy!' I quip.

"Some of the best you'll ever get!" Diva spits back rolling her neck.

"Bro!" Pat cuts in, putting us back on track.

"Check this out," I get back to the trick. "I got your address and they're getting pictures out yo' phone." I look him in the eyes as I speak to him so he'll see how serious this is.

"You make this hard for us, I'll pay your address a visit while you're still duct taped here and burn that bitch to the ground with whoever in that 'mu'fucker. And then I'm gone

46

come back here and you and me gone have some real fun."
Pat cuts in adding to the threat. "He being nice and polite.
I'm gone cut your dick off
And make you suck it."
"So you see how this work!?" I finish.
He swallows hard and nod his head unable to speak or afraid to.
"Good! We ain't gotta waste each other's time" Pat says.
"What will make it faster is if he gives us the right pin code the first go round," Diva says.
"I think he gone get it right the first go 'round," Pat said confidently.
"How you know?" Diva asks.
Wham! Just a little demonstration. I hit him in the head with the pistol. His scream is muffled by the duct tape.
"Because every time he gives a wrong number or code, I'm gone pop his ass with this pistol," I say.
As Pat gets the code I turn the TV on and tell Diva, Red and Champagne to just relax. Diva pulls out her phone and start texting. Most likely her boy Payne. Strangely I find myself feeling some type of way.
"Paradise can't wait until we finish working!" I say looking at Diva expressionless.
"Eat my pussy!" Diva fires over at me without looking up from her phone. So gutta!
"I would gladly!" I respond.
"I'm gone," Pat says preparing to leave. "I'll hit y'all up at the ATMs!"
We do our personal fly handshake of "one love" and I close and lock the door behind him. I turn back to Diva.
"Now you were saying, something about eating your pussy!"
"And you said you gladly would!" Diva said, rolling her eyes. "I bet you would if I gave you the chance."

"You would forget about the other end of that phone I know that much!" I quip.

"Uh we can hear y'all!" Red says from a corner in the room where she was chilling.

"Your point?" I ask. Her and Champagne share the same obnoxious habit of speaking at the wrong time.

"Never mind," Champagne says. See what I'm talking about?

"Naw, you right," Diva admits. "This can wait til later."

"The conversation or the texting?" I ask trying to be clear.

"Both!" she say. Ain't that a bitch. That sucks!

"I guess me and dude can talk man shit." I say putting my attention on the white dude we got tied up and naked.

"Don't pistol whip the dude cause you bored," Diva says. All of sudden she has a heart!

"Never crossed my mind!" I lie.

I walk to the bed where the dude is duct taped on and take the tape from his mouth.

"You good?" I ask.

"Yeah just a little thirsty," he answered.

"Y'all do me a favor. Give me a cup of water for our sponsor for the evening."

"Since you asked so nicely," Red said sarcastically.

"Thanks."

"At least the nigga got manners!" Diva puts in. Everybody got jokes.

"Back to you homeboy." I ignore them. "The girls see a victim in me right now. Be honest!" The dude looks at me at first trying to figure what I was up to.

"Do I look like a victim?" I ask.

"Depends," He answers hesitantly, not wanting to answer wrongly.

"Depends on what?" I ask.

"What kind of victim."

48

"A tender dick victim that softer than Charmin!" I answer.

"Well in the way you talked to them, I would say so!" He says honestly. Muthafucker could've lied.

"I don't want to talk to you no more!" I say, my pride hurt. I put the tape back over his mouth.

"Now you gone stay thirsty! Yeah, sayin' something I didn't want to hear!" I say.

"Nigga, you mean!"

Ain't this a bitch. From the bitch who set him up.

"I'm a professional!" I shoot back before Diva can speak again.

Lil Wayne's "Money on My Mind" ringtone sings from my phone.

"Get it by committee. This is young MAC speaking," I answer.

"It's all good," Pat begins. "I got one more stop to make then y'all can get out of there. The cards ran for $1500, I'm gone milk the last one to the max!"

"Where we be if you do that?" I ask.

"Over 2 stacks give or take a few hundred."

"Get at me." I say and hang up. I lean back in the chair I decided to sit in. I look around the room. I don't know if it was my silence or the way I look into everybody eyes except the dudes'. But everybody got the message.

Diva got up and start packing things up, Champagne and Red starts wiping everything down. With that being done, I ask a question.

"What kind of car he driving? "

"A grey Impala," Diva answers.

"Give me the keys," I say as I walk to her with my hand outstretched.

"You want to go by yourself and leave us here with him?" Diva asks.

"He duct taped so he good," I respond. "Matter of fact, hold

up!" I say pulling the tape out. "Let me freshen him up a
little bit!" I tape his arms to his body and I tape his legs
together at the knees. "That should hold him til I get back!"
"You want the pistol?" I ask offering the gun to Diva.
"Naw you keep it," she declines the offer. "Can I go with
you?"
I look at her. She's serious. Hell yeah! We can go anywhere
together, I think.
But I say, "Yeah come on!"
Once outside I look around the parking lot for the Impala. I
don't look long, two spaces away from the door is the car.
"Easy money!" I say, as I walk to the driver's side and direct
Diva to the trunk. "Whatever you find take it to the other
car. You or I will probably find a bag and we'll separate it
later."
"Legit!" she says.
Ten minutes later we go back to the room. We didn't find
much. But we found enough to do something with.
"That didn't take long," Diva commented.
"It usually don't. If we were at Da Lot we could really run
through that bitch!"
"What you mean?" Diva asks, not understanding.
"Like the Lexus you saw at one point. Spare tire, jacks,
carpets, lights, engine parts. Shit like that," I explain. "When
a shop won't take a car we break it down like dope on s
scale!"
Lil Wayne's "Money On My Mind" interrupts us. Right on
time!
"Speak to me," I answer.
"30 minutes," Pat says. "Have to fill up."
"No problems?" I ask.
"I'm jamming. Today is a good day right now bro," Pat
responds.
And hangs up. There's nothing left to talk about.

"It's time to go," I tell Diva and the crew. "He just lost his car."

I look at Mr. Duct-taped. "I should hogtie him so we can have a little more time."

Chapter 8

"Infamous." Champagne yells out from the front of the spot. I'm in the back.

"Yeah?" I answer.

"Diva, said it's 23 and some change."

"Is it final?" I ask.

"I don't know how she knew you would ask that," Champagne says "23.50"

"I'm, at 105.Tell Diva she can call her brother now," I say. That's met with an awkward silence. What the fuck is that all about??

"Infamous." Aww shit I know that tone and don't like it.

"Pat," I respond, knowing I won't like what's coming next.

"How do you like your news?" Pat asks. "Good, bad, or mixed!"

"Couldn't wait, could it!" I mumble.

"It's your fault," he says accusing. "You should've shot him!"

"It's always my fault. You muthafuckin' distracted me!" I shot back.

"So I'll take a piece of the blame," Pat says. "But check this out; Pain-In-The-Ass is in the parking lot and he got somebody with him."

I look up then giving him my undivided attention.

"You went through all the burners?" I ask.

"Ask another dumb question," Pat says as he passes me an all-black 9mm Ruger with a fully loaded clip.

"Where's Diva?" I ask dumbly. Pat gives me a look. Before he can say anything I throw my hand up. "Okay okay!"

I get up and we walk through the spot to the front door. At the bottom of the stairs Red and Champagne stand staring across Da Lot. I follow the direction in which they are looking. Payne and Diva are face to face having a discussion of some sort. We walk down to where Champagne and Red are standing.

"Trouble yet?" Pat asks.

"Not yet," Champagne answers.

Please don't say nothing retarded I silently pray.

"Why you didn't shoot him?" she asks.

"I couldn't find my gun!" I answer.

"You found it yet?" says Champagne.

"Only if I can use it." I noticed then the.32 I had is now in Red's small fist.

"Plan?" Pat asks as I walk towards Diva and Payne.

"Always."

As we approach Diva and Payne the other unwanted visitor gets out of the car him and Payne came in.

"Diva? I say putting my focus on her.

"What's up Infamous?" she asks.

"We got a problem!"

"Can it wait?"

"Afraid not, we need to finish our talk from earlier!" I respond.

Silence.

"Payne can I call you later?" Diva asks.

"What you mean? We talking now!" Payne says with an attitude.

54

"How he know we were back?" I ask suspiciously.

"He just drove up." I don't like that answer.

"We need a new spot," Pat cuts in.

"Can I shoot him now?" I ask in a whisper.

"What you about to do Diva?" Pat asks. "He can't sit out here all night we got too much going on!"

"Say the word." Champagne cuts in. Yep! My type of bitch.

I guess somebody said a prayer and God heard. Because just then Payne's phone sings out Lloyds "Southside" ringtone.

"You gone answer that?" Diva says studying Payne's reaction.

"It can wait," Payne answers quieting his phone.

"Who is it?" Diva asks, watching his eyes closely.

"It can wait," he says avoiding her question.

"Go handle your business so I can handle mine. Call me when you finish."

"Diva he sounds like he's ready to jump on some "Keith Sweat" type shit."

"Go ahead!" She said with finality. If it doesn't sound like goodbye to quicker ears, I don't know what does.

"You sure?" He asks, sounding like the sucker he is. For an answer, Diva just turns and gives him her back by walking away. Red and Champagne follow her. I look at Pat.

"Infamous...," sounds like a question and it was too quiet. My heater comes out at the same time as Pat's.

"We should have shot them!" Pat says not looking at me but giving "Payne in the ass" and his friend murderous looks.

"Everybody keeps tell me that!" I say with irritation.

"Hey, man I don't want no problems!" Payne says, throwing his hands up. "I'm 'bout to cut out!" Too late!

"That problem started the first time you can here!" Pat says

"Then you pop up again unannounced!" I add.

"So you got a problem regardless you want them or not!" Red says from behind us. That's what I'm talking about.

"Diva said you should have shot him!" Champagnes back too. Talk about my type of bitches! Enough said!! As if on "1" we 3 guns go off and 2 bodies fall; Payne, then his friend.

"We got about a minute and a half," I say, leading everybody away. "I hope everything is packed!"

"The bags are by the door!" Red answers.

"We taking the truck and Diva's car." Pat says and takes off running. Running behind him with Red and Champagne on our heels, I say sadly, "We saying goodbye to Da Lot !! We can't come back ever after this."

When we get to the spot Pat grabs two bags and I grab two. "You riding' with Diva?" I ask Pat. But before he can respond Diva speak.

"I'm riding with you!" she says following us out of the apartment with two bags.

"Who gone drive your car??" I ask.

"Pat." She already had plans.

"Everything packed?" Pat asks looking around at everyone.

"Everything's loaded and ready!' Champagne answers.

"Let's get the fuck out of here." I say getting into the Ford Explorer followed by Diva.

"Where we headed?" Diva asks buckling up and looking at me.

"To a real good friend. He's not that far from here!"

"We ready!" Pat hollers from Diva's car. I pull out quickly but carefully followed by Pat. We head towards Bissonnet and Beechnut. It's a hood full of white folks and Mexicans. Niggas pull through there.

"Money on my mind" sings from my phone.

"Pat?" I answer

"Smokeys?" He speaks.

"Yeah."

"Split up?"

"Yeah. I'll go lay it out first. Get back to me in 10!"

"You and Diva?" I hear something in the question but ignore it.

"In 10," I answer and he hangs up on me. I glance over at Diva.

"So," I say, not knowing how to exactly start this conversation.

"Do you want to go through the song and dance?" I ask.

"Show me what you got!" She answers.

Oh I can show her what I got alright. But that's not what she means. 10 minutes to bid for her. That's enough time to say what needs to be said

And get an understanding.

"My actions showed enough," I begin "But if you want show and tell I got you!" I say looking from the road to her and then back to the road.

"I'm all ears" she says turning in her seat so she can study me.

"Since day one I notice something unique about you." I began sincerely, "Ain't too many like you. If it was then a lot of niggas wouldn't be single." Diva just studies me as I talk so I understand what she wants "Look I'm not high on spittin game." I state looking deep in her eyes for a second or two.

"So what I say next you can take to the bank!" I say seriously." If you choose to ride with me, like I'm choosing to ride with you and for you. You won't be disappointed."

"I heard this before from other niggas" Diva responds with doubt in her voice.

"But I'm not other nigga's, I'm Infamous." I argue, looking over at her.

"You're not just some bad bitch I'm trying to recruit to show off like some trophy!"

Diva just stares at me.

"You're gonna be equal partner in everything I do. Not Bonnie & Clyde, but Diva and Infamous!" I say genuinely.
"You talking good Infamous and I want to believe You!" Diva says.
"It's not just talk. It's already proven that I'll kill for you." I say looking over into her eyes.
"When you told me you had a nigga. I knew you was gonna do two things." I say.
"And that was ?," she inquires.
"Either you was gonna set us up or you was gonna put an end to that nigga." I answer.
"So you think you on game?" Diva asks smiling.
"That's the difference between me and the niggas you used to fucking with." I say seriously.
"What's that? She asks, losing the smile.
"That ain't a game to be played this is a lifestyle a nigga live. This is what a nigga do." I say letting her know that this shit is real.
"Ain't no reset on this shit. You either win or you lose you can't redo life once it's done and over."
"What do you want from me, Infamous?" She asks. Hook Set!
"Can you drive and be driven?" I ask a question of my own! "Yeah!"
"Then be you and stay you anything else need not be said." I finish. Silence. I feel her watching my profile. Damn, not enough spoken?
"What about Pat? She finally asks. I look over at her already understanding what she's asking.
"What about him," I begin." That's my down by law brother. He gone ride with whatever is chosen by the both of us.
"I don't want this to become a problem if both of y'all like me," Diva admits.

58

"When you chose to ride with me you said a lot with that move itself. He already expects something to come." I explained. I let her chew on that for a minute. I pulled out my phone to call Smokey to get to the business. Smokey's half-black and half-white. He down like four flats. Straight ganxsta.

"Infamous." He answers my call, recognizing my number. "I ain't heard from you since the little party I had about a month ago." I put him on speaker so Diva can hear me talk.

"I been trying to do a little something." I tell him.

"If that's the case, this must be a business call," he says catching on.

"Calling for a favor and I'll pay for storage!" I explain.

"You could've came through and told me that."

"I got two loads and don't want to bring heat to your doorstep without your blessing!"

"Where are you right now?" He asks.

"Just passed grape and creeping up on your driveway." I respond "Open your garage" as I pull into the garage and hear Smokey laugh through the phone.

"What?" I ask.

"New truck? And I see something through your window!" I hang up after pulling to a stop.

Smokey comes out the house in a T-shirt and cargo shorts. He's short about 5`5` with curly blondish black hair. You can tell he's bi-racial. He has the skin complexion the color of a ripe banana. His eyes are a clear sea green.

"What's really good? I say as I pull out the first two bags.

"How much you need me to hold" he asks shaking my hand and eyeing the bags I pull out.

"12 bags!" Diva answers before I could. Smokey looks at me with a twinkle in his eye.

"My bad!" I apologize. "Diva this Smokey. Smokey this is Diva!"

"Is she taken?" He asks looking her up and down admiringly.

"Ask her," I say wanting to hear her response.

"Diva, are you single?" Smokey ask wasting no time.

"No, I'm not." She answers looking over at me." I'm with Infamous!" Guess I said something right!

"My bad, no disrespect," Smokey says throwing his hands up and frowning at me.

"Don't worry about it. I'm just finding out myself." I tell Smokey.

Chapter 9

"Pappy said he'll check Da Lot and see if the cars still there" Smokey says hanging up the phone. I ran down the whole play to him. Most of it anyway. Now we all were gathered at his house.

"He gone take care of them?" I ask." We just want to sell the engines in them!" Pat cuts in.

"That's it?" Smokey asks.

"It's only 3 plus the Explorer. Tell him he can have the discount at 5 a piece," I answer.

"I'll see what's up!" Smokey responds. As he picks up the phone, Pat looks at me.

"Infamous," Pat calls

"Pat," I say mockingly. We continue

"We still ain't split the score," I say.

"Will or Frank?" Pat asks.

"I was thinking of your cousin," I posit.

"Sonja or Scuda?" Pat asks.

"My bad, your auntie" Pat says.

"We'll have to…" I stop aww shit.

"Exactly."

"Are we part of this in any way?" Champagne cuts in and

asks.

"Yeah, cause y'all got some shit goin' on with this on one accord type shit," Diva adds.

"Ride for a while like we have and shit just happens like that," Pat says.

"They always say great minds think alike anyway!" I say.

"So what was this exactly about?" Red asks wanting to know the scoop.

"His G-Momma stays with his auntie, and she ain't green to this lifestyle. We gone have to let her put her price on what we got," Pat explains. Meaning she gone want a cut and she'll vouch for us with my auntie."

"The plus side is we won't have to rush nothing, and I get to see my cousin Kristi."

"I don't see a problem." Diva says naively.

"You ain't heard her price yet." I say preparing myself for a mental wrestling match.

...

"Momma, you serious," I ask while over my Auntie's house. I already knew it was gon' be some crucial shit. We done drove from the Southwest to Cullen and Orem on the Southeast for my momma to get crazy.

"If you really sittin' on 128 grand, you lucky I ain't hit you in yo head for the 20," my mamma says sitting across from me on the couch in pink sponge rollers and a house coat.

My mom and I share the same black as midnight skin tone as me. She still has a youthful figure.

"I'm cool with the price! "Diva says she just had to open her mouth!

"Us too "Champagne says speaking for her and Red.

I look over at Pat.

"Pat" I say.

"Infamous." He answers sarcastically.

"A little help," I say needing him right now.

62

"15 is a good number," Pat said not being any help at all. I'm glad that we were paying Smokey with what came of cars in Da Lot.

"Aight," I say after a couple of seconds. "But that should cover our next couple of trips."

"Why you always want to give me a hard time?" Momma complains.

"Cause he know I get a kick out of seeing y'all go at it!" Pat cuts in.

"So this happens every time they link up?" Diva asks being nosy.

"Just about," Pat answers. "Sometimes we be in a rush and can't really push and pull."

"Momma, where Kristi at?" I ask getting up now that business is over.

"She might be on the phone." Momma answers getting up too.

"Go see while I talk to Carla."

"I'm gonna go find her," I say. "Pat put my cut back in the pot."

I know if my little cousin is on the phone and not in her bedroom then she's in the kitchen. So I make my way down the hallway. I pass the two bedrooms. I see she's not there. In the kitchen, Kristi's sitting at the dining room table giggling and whispering into the phone.

"Who you on the phone with little girl," I ask surprising the shit out of her.

She jumps up looking like a cat eating the canary and just stares at me.

"Hello… Earth to Venus," I say snapping my fingers in her face.

"I'll call you back," she says into the phone, "Cousin!" where you been? You ain't been over here in forever!" says Kristi.

"I was just over here a few months ago," I respond.

"Pat with you?" she asks looking behind me.

"Yeah. He in the garage," I answer. "I got some friends with me too?"

"Who," she asks, walking towards the garage. We pass my aunt's bedroom. My mom comes out and gives the green light to set up a temporary spot in the garage. Kristi stops at the door to the garage.

And looks back at me.I thought she had forgotten. Whenever I'm here the garage is off limits unless she gets permission from me or Pat. She looks and smiles.

"Can I go in?" She asks.

"You remember the rule?"

"Look but don't touch," she answers. "Okay"

When she opens the door, I expect her to just go in. But she hesitates. I nod. This is the most we've ever brought to this house and put in the garage, so I understand her hesitation.

"What's up baby girl? Pat speaks

"Heeeyyy!!" Kristi runs and jumps on him.

"I don't even get a welcome like that and I'm family!" I say, a little jealous.

"You ain't me!" Pat says with his chest slightly poked out.

"I'm her cousin!" I say

"My point exactly," Pat says.

"Who are they? Y'all girlfriends," she asked, looking towards Champagne, Red, and Diva.

Only youngsters can get away with questions like that.

"That's Diva, the chocolate one. She with me!" I began.

"That's Champagne and Red. They with Pat."

Oh yeah, you think!" Diva responds playfully. I give her a look. This Diva is too cool.

"We with Pat," Champagne asks, not liking the way that sounded.

Kristi just stands there with her mouth wide open. She's not

64

used to seeing us bringing anybody around. Since they are there she knows something is going on.

"I think we should tie Infamous up and beat him!" Pat offers.

"Hey, I'm right here! What's up with this shit," I say.

"I second that." Diva says giving me a playful mischievous look

"Since he think I'm with him," she adds.

"Hey do I get a say?" I ask.

"Is it anymore duct tape?" Champagne asks. Sure glad ever body in a festive mood!

"You'll hurt me in front of my cousin." I look over at Kristi for help.

"Just don't kill him please!! Kristi says and everybody laughs. Ain't that a bitch!

"I like Kristi," Diva says walking over to Kristi and giving her a hug

"Us too," Champagne adds as Red nods. What's this shit? We all one big happy family.

"That's my baby." Pat informs. I slide out of the garage while everybody distracted and run into Auntie Carla.

"What's up C?" I say as I give her a big hug, "Eric wants to talk to you about something, but he won't tell me what it's about," Carla says.

Last time I talked to Eric, I damn near got fucked off in South Park. Another Southeast hood!

"Where he at, "I ask not really wanting to talk to him. I know Eric was on some rah rah shit. I was ready to get this money I didn't need no setbacks for no dumb shit.

"He's in the backyard." she answered walking off.

Before I could walk off to the backyard, Diva pops up surprise! "We really need to talk, she begs.

…

Sitting in the car, we turn the radio on and at first we sit in a comfortable silence gathering our thoughts. She's the one that asked for this but I am the one that first breaks the silence.

"Diva I already know what your heart has chosen so you can be easy. I'm not gone fuck over you! I began. We lock eyes and I watch as all doubt melts away. As if pulled by a strong magnetic primal force she throws herself on me and our lips lock into a passionate kiss. I hear her soft moan of pleasure and I growl deep in my throat.

"Damn, girl!" I say breathing heavy.

"If this was a movie, then I'd say some extra romantic shit," I glance around outside the car and I see no one. "But this is real life so I'm gone stay on some real shit. Get in the back seat and get naked," I order her sexy ass. Hesitating she jumps in the backseat and comply. We need some mood music to set the stage for this shit. I hit a couple of buttons and "Lollypop" by Lil Wayne comes through the speaker. Jumping in the backseat, I kiss her deeply while my hands fly all over her body. She says, "It feels like you got 8 hands," My hands are everywhere at once. Her body so thick but her skin is so soft. I'm sucking on her lips and squeezing her nipples. I feel them harden under my fingertips. I look into her eyes. She looks so soft and vulnerable now. I place my warm mouth where my now wet fingers just were just sucking and biting on her nipples. She arches her back and I can feel her shiver." Aahh shit!" she moans as I kiss down to her navel cavity. I rub her honey spot and feel that she's soaking wet from the inside. She ready for me. But still I take my time. When I reach the V between her thighs I inhale the fragrance of her arousal. I smell her natural scent. Damn this bitch is driving me wild! "I'm about to taste you," I whisper as I kiss her second set of lips. Her legs spread wide as she grabs my head. I'm running my tongue up and down her fatty folds. I

66

take my thumb and forefinger and search for that men in the boat. There he is. I found him. I feel Diva tense up and then gasp. I lap at her clitoris like a kitten lapping at sweet warm milk.

"Oh God oh God!" she moans as her thick thigh clamps tight around on my head. I suck on her button.

"Shii…aww shiii… shiii…," Diva starts to sake and flop like a fish. Quickly I cover her mouth with my hand because I know…

"Ahhhhhhhh!!!!!" she screams. I knew that was coming But I can't help that I'm not through. I add more pressure to her clit. "Cum baby cum!" I whisper.

"Awww shit aww shiiit!"She sweating and breathing heavy as she lays there on the back seat, her eyes closed tight.

"You and I momma!" I say kissing her between her thighs. I give her a little time to recuperate. I unzip my pants and I pull my hardness out I don't think it'll be wise for me to get naked "sssssss" she hisses as I slowly glide inside of her.

"Can you handle me baby? "I ask as she just nods her head. Her eyes remain closed.

Damn! She's so tight. I slide back and forth trying to work my chubby 9$^{1/2}$-inch dick inside her.

"Damn daddy," she moans slowly. I work my hips. She's so tight, its mmmmmm-good.

"Sssss!" she breathes I feel her opening up for me accommodating my size. "Ooh shit!" she moans. I push all the way in and pause loving the feeling of the warmth and wetness of her.

"Damn, Diva girl!" I say and started working the magic stick. I listen to the wet smacking sounds our bodies makes and get turned on even more.

"Take and claim this pussy," Diva moans matching me thrust for thrust. >I bit her neck and fuck her. The car rocks heard as I get in rhythm

"You know what it is right!?" I ask pulling her hair and fucking her wildly.

"Tell me daddy!" she digs her nails into my back

"You fuck up I'll kill you!!" I say driving into her.

"Oh, oh, uh I'm 'bout to cum. Awwww!!!" Diva screams out. Her teeth clamp onto my shoulders and she squeezes me as we both explode. "Oh shit!"

…

"What it do, 'E," I ask walking into the backyard. E is standing by the gate smoking a blunt and texting. "E" was my uncle. His real name was Edward, but we had been calling him "E" for as long as I can remember. He was about 5'9, Dirty Red with freckles.

"What's good nephew?!" He walked over and gave me dap.

"Carla said you need to holla at me!" I responded getting right to the point. Even though 'E' was family, I didn't really like fucking with him on really any type of level with him as it was almost always some bullshit.

"You got a little free time," He asks, looking at me.

"Depends," I answer carefully."

"Da Lot still open for business?

"Just got burned today," I say frowning "And I gotta find a new spot to unload just then Pat walked into the backyard to join us and calls me out.

"Infamous?"

"Haven't gotten their yet." I respond "What's the deal E?"

"I need y'all skill set! "It didn't take no genius to figure that.

"Just tell 'em" momma says. Where the hell did she come from?

"Pat" I say making sure he was paying attention I didn't like the way momma just popped out of nowhere and how she was sounding.

"Remember South Park," E asks. I knew it was some bullshit.

68

Chapter 10

As I lean the chair back against the wall in the garage, I watch everybody's reaction as Pat gives the rundown on our new South Park situation. I say nothing and just listen to everyone else's feedback. I need to see how the rest of the team responds. Kristi was told to leave the garage because this was some shit she didn't need to know and be no party to. She knew what Pat, me, momma, and everybody did and we don't lie to her about nothing. She's even been to Da Lot and Smokey's a few times.

I notice it's silent around me

"What?" I ask noticing everybody looking at me.

"You too quiet!" Red says studying me.

"No he's not." Pat responds" That's the Infamous I'm used to

Right now he's doing a lot of thinking."

"I'm always thinking "I defend.

"Is there a picture I'm not getting," Diva cuts in

"Any way!" Red interrupts the small talk." What we gone do snd what's the plan?

Red is talking from a sofa that sits against the wall in the garage. Red's about that action and not playing no games.

"I got to call Smokey back," I say.

"But you don't want to use him," Pat cuts in. I nod at Pat to let him knows he was correct.

"PR and Lil 50," he asks. I look around at Diva, Red, Champagne. I studied each one of them to see if they were built for this shit; really ready and willing for some gutta shit. True enough they were some street hoes who had been around the block a time or two. But being from the streets and getting gutta was two different things.

"Why do y'all gotta get somebody else," Red says breaking the silence.

"All y'all need y'all got with y'all two, me Champagne, And Diva," she adds.

I look at Champagne and Diva to see their reaction to what Red says. Then my eyes turn to Pat who's looking at me with 2 questions in his eyes.

"I think they ready," I respond to the question in his eyes. I know we 'bout to get into some gutta shit. The last time we went in we went in lightly. Now we 'bout to put so much weight on this shit. Sympathy and empathy is getting packed and sent away to another galaxy.

"The deal is though we gone need 2 fresh cars," I explain as I lay out the plan.

I know everything needs to be on point. I also know the chemistry that Pat and me have with this shit is lined and defined.

We've only hit one lick with Red, Champagne, and Diva. Even though that one went off smoothly, that doesn't mean that any others will go the same. I ponder if this is the time to test that and take that chance?

...

Since you and Diva think y'all gone be the next Bonnie & Clyde, y'all gone be the drivers on this shit." Pat says.

"So who gone ride with who, Champagne asks. The only thing that makes sense is Red riding with me and Pat with

70

Diva. Champagne is the odd women out. But since she's an extension of Red, I know she's gone end up in the car with me and her girl.

"Y'all good," I ask, looking from Diva to Pat. We don't need no complications. I don't know how Pat feels about the situation between me and Diva yet. I know he had felt some type of way for Diva too. Earlier, when we had returned from the little rendezvous in the backseat of the car, I see that Pat was on to us. Even though his facial expression didn't portray his feelings, I could see something in his eyes just wasn't alright for a second or two. I was hoping it was just my imagination. Pat nodded his head and looked at Diva.

"You ain't trippin' that you won't be up under yo' boyfriend for a minute," he says to Diva.

"I'm a grown ass woman and 'bout my business," Diva says rolling her eyes. Before
any tension could set in, I change the subject.

"We all gone ride to the stroll in the Galant and move from there," I say as the plan of attack.

"Let's ride!" Red says getting up. That chick is about action.

…

On the way to the stroll, we're rolling. Everybody lost in their own thoughts. Diva's driving. We haven't spoken about what happened in the backseat that is now occupied by Pat, Champagne and Red. I hope she's not sitting over in the driver seat now regretting our dogging episode. I'm not a tender dick weak nigga, but our session had me feeling some type of way. My thoughts are interrupted by a text notification. Before I could check my phone, Pat wants to know who it is.

"So," Pat asks.

"Scuda," I answer.

"What he want?" Pat probes.

"E called him and he wants to help."

"Who is Scuda," Diva cuts in, turning the music down.

"A monster with no conscience," I say thinking about Scuda. Scuda's mentality is with them hard, so they don't or can't hit back.

Fucking with Scuda you going to hell with gasoline draw's on!!

"We don't need no help." Red speaks up from the back I'm liking the bitch 'get down.' But still there's so much to still be seen.

Scuda says he wants to blow that bitch up and be done with it! I bring him back to reality. "That can't happen!"

"Infamous always wants to profit from shit. That's how he got in the last situation," Pat says complaining.

"We need some more duct tape," I say ignoring Pat. It is what it is.

"We good! We do need to call Smokey though," I say and go to my phone.

"Something ain't right. You callin' me twice in one night," Smokey says, answering the phone.

"Can you do a pick up?" I ask.

"Who car and where?" he queries.

"Diva's on Hillcroft & 59," I share.

"When?" he agrees. I can always count on Smokey.

"Give me a second and I'll call you when I got there." I respond and hang up. Diva glances over at me in the passenger seat. She has a frown on her face.

"Shouldn't we scope the place out first?" she asks wisely.

"Because they know Infamous and they know me," Pat cuts in.

"We not really walking in blind. We know what the whole lay out is," says Diva.

"Just trust that we know what we doin'," I add.

"It's gone be like a kick door, but we leaving no witnesses,"

72

I say locking eyes with her.

"My cousin Scuda would be good for this. But y'all say y'all ready so here we is!" I look back first at Red, then Champagne. I nod to Pat. They're ready!

"Pat, roll us one," I say, ready for some weed.

"You sure this is a good time?" Pat asks.

"I really want a X!" I say.

"One blunt comin' right up," Pat approves. As we hit Taft, Tupac's "Hail Mary," sings from Pat's phone.

"What it do?" I hear him answer. Now we got some other shit poppin' off. But we gon' fuck with y'all later." Pat hangs up. I give him a look to share.

"P.A. and Lil' 50!" he says before I have to ask him. "They want us to get up with them later," Pat says.

Chapter 11

The last time I was there with E's son, it was some bullshit. When me and E rolled up, his son was beat down bad. E being a thoroughbred veteran ganxsta nigga jumps right out the car and left me reaching for the pistol. By the time I do get to the action, E done beat 2 niggas senseless. While they were out, e being the get money nigga I am, I rifle through the pockets of the two dudes that's out cold. They didn't have nothing, but a couple of hundred dollars. But free money was free money.

No one told me the real issue though. E didn't inform me that the reason that they was getting at his boy was because he owed them many. As I reach my car door, the gun shots began. As I open the door, I felt a hot pain go across my back. I hollered like a bitch and fell into the car seat. I shoot wildly while trying to strengthen up and get the car moving. E and his son get into the car. But before I can pull off, a bullet shatters the window on the passenger side. I roll out of there as quickly as possible. The crazy part is the fact that E's boy jumped out on some pain freak shit because he went back. He waited a while but still... When he returned they pistol whipped him and left him for dead. Still niggas want they bread!!

Fat Joe's "Lean Back" snaps me out of my thoughts.

"When we get off the freeway pull up at "Jack-n-the Box," I tell Diva turning down the music.

"On foot from there?" Pat asks. I nod at him.

"Call Smokey cause we'll be there in a few minutes!" I tell Pat.

It takes 2 rings for him to pick up.

"Where you at?" I hear Smokey ask. The car seems extra quiet.

"59 and Hillcroft at the 'Jack-n-the Box!" Pat answers.

"I got the tow truck, so just leave it there." Smokey replies.

'Done!" I respond. I look at Diva. She has her eyes on something in front of us. As we go under the freeway. I notice the Jack-n the Box is kind of full for a Wednesday night. When we pull into the lot, I look at the shell gas station on the corner. It's next to the Wells Fargo and the Best Western is next to it. There is nothing average about a hoe stroll on Da West.

"How about we catch two at the shell at the same time and be done with it," Pat suggests.

"That could work, but Diva gotta be able to keep up with me," I remind. I lost her last time.

"I caught up with you!" Diva defends.

"Only cause I slowed down and waited," I make clear.

"Bet a hundred you won't lost me this time," Diva challenges.

"And to make it sweeter, the winner gets a full body massage," Fuck the money, I'll take the message like King Kong roaring I think to myself.

"Diva you remember the last time I told you don't do it?" Pat interrupted. Damn won't he shut up sometimes.

"Make it a thousand and a full spoil and you got a bet!" Pat says.

"What's a full spoil?" Champagne asks.

76

"It's like goin' to the spa, only it's bubble baths, blunts, body massages, the works." Pat explains.

"A Valentine's Day only the movies look fly." I say. I'm already planning on losing the bet as we talk. I need that from Diva. I want to put her under my spell. I start thinking about our little time together earlier. Wasn't anything gentle about how we got down. I really want to show my skills. Show her there's more to my persona than the hustler, gangsta, pimp

lifestyle that I live.

"Take your time before you answer," I warn Diva.

"Make it light on yourself." Diva studies me for a minute.

"Why does it seem like this happens a lot," Red cuts in. Sometimes this bitch picks a hell of a time to open her mouth.

"It doesn't!" I say immediately. Killing that before it even begins.

"All Diva has to do is keep up." Red says

"Diva?" I speak

"Where we headed again!!" Diva locked it in on her phone.

…

Before you know it we're off. I'm in a '03 Chevy Monte Carlo. Behind me is Diva in a '94 Nissan 240. The Nissan fits Diva perfectly. It's small and fire engine Red. The Monte Carlo is the color of champagne. The average trip from 59 and Hillcroft to the King's Flea Market is about 15-20 minutes away tops depending on if you keep the speed limit. I keep Diva in my rearview, but I make it seem like I'm really trying to shake her. I know Pat telling Diva right now that I could lose her anytime I want to. Most folks take 610, forgetting that 288 gets closer to the flea market.

"Are you really into Diva?" Red breaks the silence. I glance at her and then at Champagne. "What's this? What kind a question is that?" I ask, not answering her question immediately.

"Diva is my girl, she done been through so much with niggas." Red says, looking me straight in the eye. I feel her scrutiny. I'm not afraid of this questioning. But where would it lead. I don't know her reason for wanting to know and I don't know what she'll do with the information she wants to get from me.

"Man, I'm a street nigga and I love down bitches and thoroughbred hoes. Diva's both!" I say. Red studies me for a minute, then she looks back at Champagne.

"I don't do games. Plus, now I'm on some other level shit. Diva is my type of hype wrapped in pure, genuine high-quality diamonds." I say, pouring all the passion I can muster in my voice. Although there was really no need because I was really feeling some type of way for Diva. But I knew this conversation would be repeated, and analyzed, dissected and weighed later. That's just what type of species women are. I knew I had to play this carefully.

"You niggas go to trippin' when a bitch shows you she's really down for y'all you start getting big headed. Thinking a bitch will just allow herself to get drug through the mud." Champagne cuts in.

"It's like you niggas are wired backward and zigzagged and all crooked," she and Red shared a laugh on that one. I could tell Red and Champagne was two women scorned. That's why they were probably the way they were. A lot of females say being messed over by dudes ain't always the reason. The shit too confusing for me to try and ever figure out!

"I'm a different breed of nigga!" I defend. I lock eyes with both of them to let 'em see my sincerity.

"Me and the niggas y'all use to don't even white associate in the same mental space." These hoes done put me in my Preacher Pimpin' Ken shit. I go all the way in.

78

"It ain't no gimmick with me. If I ain't on you, then fuck you. Ain't no pretending. If I wanted to just fuck that's what I would say!" I finish. Through the silence the follows, I know the speech I gave them has them sold. I smile inside.

Chapter 12

I turn into the Walgreens parking lot smiling inside. I did my best to show
Diva that by me losing the bet, she won the time of her life. By the way that I fucked
her earlier maybe she wanted to lose on purpose too. Shid, two could play the reverse double clutch game. Diva pulls in behind me a minute or so later. But the celebration is gone be short-lived because its business that need to be handled.

"It's 11:26 p.m on a school night." I say to everybody around me.

"The last time I just ran in not taking my time peeping everything," I continue.

"This niggas so dramatic," Pat says interrupting and making light of the situation.

"We passed the spot we gone hit and he saw something he didn't like!" Pat adds.

"I told y'all he turned on me." I say half-jokingly.

"Anyway it was still some lights on and I want to catch them in bed with they pants down!" I add.

"You should call Scuda," Pat says.

"It's not that bad!" I respond defensively I don't know why

all of a sudden he doubting my skills. Pat goes quiet. Okay, this might be the time to listen to him. Maybe he knows something that I don't know or feel something that he can't put into words.

"Aight, I'll call scuda" I relent. Everybody turns and look at me.

"It's your call," Pat says. Really it ain't!

"We don't need Scuda, we got Red," I say and everybody looks at me bewildered.

"All we need is what we got here, let's ride!" I say, putting my foot down.

Parked across the street, in front of Hartfield Elementary the house is totally dark. Pat and me were already in position to go through the backdoor. Diva is parked at the front of the house. Her and the girls ready to set it off eye-candy style." Not a car in right and not a cricket chirping. All of a sudden, Boom! We crash the doors from front to back almost simultaneously, like rounding cattle up we had these 4 dudes face down in no time. This shit is almost too easy. Me and Pat make quick world with the duct tape. The only problem was we hadn't planned how we were gonna get these four bodies, to the car in one move. Impossible! I was wondering which two girls could carry a body. Diva was stallion thick by the thighs and bubble butt-ly big in the ass, but her muscles wouldn't allow her to handle no full grow man. Red and Champagne are the same way.

"Hey Diva, Champagne, Red, y'all take the house. Turn this motherfucker upside down quickly as you can. Me and Pat gone deal with the bodies," I order.

We escort them weak and dazed with duct tape over their mouth to the awaiting Monte Carlo. Just as we got them all situated in the car, Lil Webbie's song, "Bad Bitch" starts singing from my phone.

"I bet y'all out there cracking jokes while we sit in here and do all this hefty lifting," Diva says into the phone.

"On the way momma," I cut in. There was no need to get into that argument right now. We left the bodies and I kicked open the door. In the front room there were three trash cans full of good green medicine. The smell is so strong you can damn near get high from the scent alone.

"What the fuck," I start wide-eyed at some unbelievable shit. "Did I walk into a dream come true?"

"It's 3 different types too!" Diva says unable to disguise the excitement in her voice.

"What's this shit worth?" Champagne asks, seeing major dollar signs.

"Shid, it could be up to 9G's a piece. That's if the can holds up to 30 lbs," I figure.

"Since y'all seen that, come look at this shit we got in here!" Red yells, pulling us into a bedroom. The mattress to the bed is flipped over and cut open. I don't have to see no more.

"Why we still looking at this shit and not loading up!" I say as everybody starts to move with purpose.

"Infamous" Diva calls. I pause about to get frustrated. Time is of the essence and they act like we got a lifetime.

"Diva" I say.

"They got a safe" she says matter-of-factly.

"We don't have time for that we need to move quick," I say.

"Too bad," Pat say cutting in. Damn where did that come from. Pat don't start tripping on me now. One after another we go around arguing, wasting time and losing money.

"I'll be outside on lookout this gone take a while," I say, breaking down.

I want to be gone and out the way, but we got 3 trash cans full of good weed, a lot of cash, and it look like they want to be greedy.

Chapter 13

I been outside for at least 30 minutes bored out of my muthafucking mind. These niggas in the backseat keep moaning and moving trying to get loose. I played whack-a-mole with my gun on them for about 5 minutes, but that got boring too. I see Pat coming out of the house with 2 black garbage bags. He dropped the bags right on the porch and stepped back in the door a grabbed a bag big enough to put a body in. I pop the trunk. Get out and rush to the porch to help load some stuff up. After loading up the two cars we take off. When Diva got in the car she was carrying a big Prada purse.

"Where you get that from?" I ask.

"They had it in one of the bedrooms. It's brand new. I guess somebody bought it for their girlfriend or momma!" Diva says.

"Guess they'll never get it," I respond. I put Lil' Wayne's "Tha Carter III" in the deck. The song "Got Money" with T. Pain blasts from the speakers. We take Griggs to Cullen for a straight shot back to my Auntie's crib. I turn the radio down.

"Call my Auntie C on my phone and put it on speaker," I say, tossing Diva my phone. We had switched up after coming out of the house. It was some natural automatic unspoken shit. Now Champagne and Red was riding with Pat and Diva was once again riding with me. Now we were comfortable and in sync.

"Problem?" Diva asks looking for reassurance.

"Semi," the phone rings over the speaker. Auntie C picks up.

"Can you get E on the line please," Diva says into the phone before I can say anything. It gets silent on the other end.

"It's cool Auntie!" I speak up. I can sense my auntie's hesitation.

"Hold on," she responds." He in the backyard," she says. I really need to get his new cell phone number I ponder.

"Hello!" E's voice comes over the speaker.

"We goin to a funeral," I say

"Am I invited?" E asks speaking code.

"No but you can call Scuda and tell him he can party like it's New Year's if he want. I left a couple of presents at the house for somebody. In the garage, there's a truck and a bad ass bike!" I say.

"I'll be sure to tell him that!" E says as we end the call.

"So what we gone do with them? Diva asks, wondering the fate of the dudes in the backseat duct-taped and laid out cold.

"We gone make a bonfire and roast marshmallows," I respond. She frown at me confused "Homemade cremation," I say to her confusion.

"First, we gone go unload the cars at auntie C house!"

...

I back the Monte Carlo into the garage. Pat already done unloaded his car. I have to hurry and unload the goods and the bodies. I don't want to get caught with neither. After unloading the stuff in the garage, Pat and me sat in the car with the bodies. I know we made a mistake by keeping the bodies.

We should have put the bodies in the house and went 'Scuda' on they ass. Uupp!

That's when the light bulb pops off in my mind. Just then, trick Daddy's "I'm a Thug" sings out from my phone.

"You must have been readin' my mind," I say into the phone.

"When you think dark thoughts it's like a telepathic message to me!" Scuda said sounding sinister.

'Y'all take care of y'alls situation in South Park," I asked. It must be these niggas destiny to burn!

"We got four lost sinners that need to pay for their transgressions," I say. What's spooky about this shit is as soon as I said what I said to Scuda, I could feel a weird type of excitement coming through the phone.

"You want my specialty," Scuda responded quickly. I look over at Pat and he smiles at me." Of course," I say.

"We can meet where you choose," I end the call.

…

After watching Scuda burn those bodies and smelling the sickening stench of burning human flesh for the first time, I'm left with a weight on me. Not only that, but that shit put a strange smell in your nostrils and leaves a strange taste in your mouth. We were all back at Auntie C's. I' m puffing hard on a blunt, trying to get that strange taste out of my mouth and the shit off my mind. Somebody had found some big speakers and set up a backyard mini-party. I guess the feeling of success after accumulating some funds gives you the party vibes." I guess everybody feels euphoric when they make some money!

"How we gone divide this shit up?" Red asks, reading everybody minds. That's what I love and hate about this bitch: her boldness. But sometimes she just needs to shut the fuck up!

"Do we have to discuss that shit now?" I ask, mad that this bitch gone fuck up the festive vibes. Money seems to almost always cause problems, especially when you dealing with family and so-called friends.

"Better to get the shit settled and out the way!" Red says. I looked over at Pat and he looked up at me. Usually this shit was easy because it was just me and Pat. We didn't have to divide profit because we was eating together. We ate off the same plate and we drunk from the same cup. Now we dividing shit up.

"We got to fuck wit' the smoke man," I say talking about Smokey and his assistance with the work.

"Didn't you give him the address so he could go back and get the truck and the bikes?" Red asks.

"What that mean?" I say frowning. That don't pay him for what we already owe. The truck and the bikes were extra. I watched as Red and Champagne shared a glance. On the table in front of Champagne was money and jewelry. I noticed a nice watch I would like to rock, but didn't mention it.

"Let's divide up the money first!" Diva says, clearing the air.

"I don't know how we gone get an even split out of all this," Pat complained. I looked at him funny. The tone of voice had didn't sound like the usually Pat.

"How not," I say.

"We gone be short. It ain't gone be enough bread to feed a baby Chee Chee!" Again I frowned at Pat. All the stuff we had retrieved from the house: the dope, the guns, the jewelry and the money. It was a successful night. Plus, added with the first we were straight. I felt it was more than the money that Pat had an issue with. I noticed a strange type of vibe between he and Diva. I don't know what happened in their little ole car ride to South Park. But something with them was now off.

"Pool my money with yours!" Dive said to me.

"That figures!" Pat said sarcastically. Diva and me exchanged a look. So did Champagne and Red. I guess it was ok! Official! Auntie C, momma and E had gotten everything they need settled and drifted back into the house. It was Champagne, Red, Diva, me and Pat, we needed to get off the weed and the jewelry then we'd know where we all stood.

"Diva, you gon' call your brother!" I asked.

"Already done," I say, looking at Pat.

"You get a connect for the jewelry right Pat," I ask. He nods his head without looking at me. Look like he was playing on his phone. I'm really trying to figure out what his deal is.

"My brother ready for us," Diva said before I could dwell too long on Pat's unexplained behavior.

"Let's load 2 of the trash cans into the car," I say getting up and heading to the garage. I look back at Pat and he hadn't moved.

"You and Diva take care of that. I'm about to go fuck with the jewelry," He said and walked in the opposite direction. I'm wondering what's wrong with this nigga and what to do about it. How in the hell Diva gonna help me put two trash cans in the trunk! Oh well!

"You ready," I say looking up her up and down as flashbacks of our backseat rendezvous creep into my mind.

…

We're all in the car. Diva driving, I'm in the passenger seat and Red and Champagne in the back. Shawanna's "Getting Some Head" was playing on the speakers. Everybody was in their vibe or at least I thought they were.

"I think Pat getting jealous," Red said out loud. A fact I didn't want to admit.

"Naw, my nigga don't stress over no pussy!" I defended.

"Oh now, I'm just pussy" Diva said with an attitude.

"I didn't mean it like that, but you know what I'm talking about." I say, trying to clean up the mess my mouth was about to get me into.

"No, I don't... Explain!" she says looking at me with a side eye and a neck roll.

"Me and that nigga go back since hush puppies and jellys!," I say bringing up old school staple shoes.

"There's 3 things that can and will always change nigga's. That's money, pussy, and time," Red stated matter-of-factly. That was some truth she spit for real.

"Real nigga's stay real. Time doesn't erode a genuine artifact," I say.

"That shit sound good and poetic nigga. But a nigga is born with human nature and that means flaws and ugly shit. I listened to what Diva said, and she wasn't lying at all. I just didn't want to believe that Pat was switching up on a nigga.

"See y'all ain't use to no real authentic nigga's," I defended, "Y'all don' trust nobody!"

"Experience has taught us that nigga's ain't shit," Champagne cut in. She and
Red were wrapped up in the back seat like two snakes.

"Experience is the best and the worst teacher," Red added.

"People reveal and show their true colors. Where words fail, actions don't lie. Damn, these chicks have really been through the ringer. They on some 'When a woman fed up' type-shit.

"Why y'all riding down on my nigga like that?" I ask looking back at Red and Champagne.

"We just stating facts!" they retort collectively.

"Money on my mind" sings in from my phone. And a strange hush just comes over the car.

"Pat" I confirm. "You havin' fun yet." I ask him. It's like every eye in the car is one me and Pat's voice is extra loud on the phone. I look straight ahead.

"Tryin to get this shit together, what's up?" I respond into the phone ignoring what he just said.

"Well I got 3 for all the jewelry. I tried to get more since we splitting this shit 5 ways," Pat says.

"We'll be alright!" I say, thinking maybe Red's talk was getting to me because I felt a crazy vibe coming from Pat through the phone. Or maybe I was just imagining things. This was my nigga. We had tossed hoes like nutritious nuts and salads. How could he be feeling some type of way off some pussy he's never sampled I wondered.

"We on our way to see Diva's brother now," I share with Pat.

"Remember, it's bro's before hoes!" Pat says and hangs up. Where did that come from. That's a hell-of-a way to end a phone call. I glance back at Red and Champagne. They done tuned the world out and was making out like lovebirds in the backseat. I looked over at Diva who didn't seem to be paying attention to nothing but the road and our destination.

Chapter 14

3 weeks later we were at an apartment that Diva and I had rented together. I needed a place to duck off to and me and Diva was getting real serious. We had been hitting licks together on some Bonnie and Clyde-type shit. Pat had took some of the weed we had and opened up a weed spot. Then he got a new connect through Diva's brother. So far, Pat was pulling in some real money. He was still my nigga though and my feelings hadn't changed despite our tension. I still fucked with him the same way I had before Diva. I had been by his pot on several occasions. I had even tried to get him to go on a few capers with me and Diva. His excuse was he was trying to establish his spot in the weed game. I was still that jack of all trades. Mostly though me and Diva was setting up big money dope boys. We purchased a place in Shatoe off of Homestead. With the money we made we fully furnished the apartment with leather and glass.

…

Laying in our bedroom on the unmade bed, I was in my birthday suit while Diva, smoking a blunt and watching the big screen lay in a pink lace bra and panties, looking like a scene out of a Rudy Ray Moore movie. She was watching John Singleton's "Baby Boy" with Tyrese and Taraji P

Henson. They were on the scene where Tyreese was eating pussy. Diva looked over at me with that look in her eyes. I smiled, knowing what was coming next.

"I don't know why you given me those eyes," I said as Diva licked her lips, turning me all the way on. She ran a manicured hand between her legs and before I knew it a tentpole appeared down below.

"Let me hit that," I demanded. Before I was two puffs in, Diva had a mouth full of my chubby 9½ inches.

"Shiittt, girl," I moan. Damn she bad! She slowly took a couple of more inches of me into her warm, wet mouth. My toes curled and my hands gripped the sheets. I bit my bottom lip and let out a, "aww... fuck," cursing in pleasure, loving the blow job I getting as sensations were felt all over my body. Diva looked at me the whole time. Using her hands, tongue, neck rolls and mucho spit, this was the height of a good time for me. She had me calling out to every God and demi-God in the universe. I'm sure I was speaking in tongues before I lost all control.

After swallowing, she came up smacking her lips and smiling. All I could do is lay there and try to catch my breath. Damn. I love this bitch!

...

"Hey, Red and Champagne got a lick for us," Diva said knowing how to cap some shit off. Two things a man love the most. Head and some money!

"Let me see if Pat wants part of that action," I say getting up from the bed grabbing my phone.

"You know he ain't gonna get down, so why do you keep asking," Diva said as she lay on the bed.

"Cause that's still my nigga and I gotta give him the option to decline," I say and walked into the shower. Pat had been distancing himself from me and Diva was over it. But I thought it was because he was just trying a new hustle. I

94

didn't want to believe that he was distancing himself because of jealously. He didn't even call like he used to. But I was also doing my thing too. Me and Diva had began moving as a team. But I never did forget about Pat. He was always a part of my thoughts and plans. He the one that always chose to decline the offers to get money. I always thought about him though and called him to when an opportunity presented itself. In the past week or so though, I hadn't called him as much. As I showered and thought about the situation with me and Pat, I got emotional. We used to be inseparable. A nigga didn't want to jump on no female shit and feel some type of way about him, but I did. If he was moving solo because he was feeling some type of way about Diva and my relationship then that was something else entirely. I realized I needed to talk to him. Instead of assuming I needed to listen to what he had to say and clear the air. Find out what the nigga was going through. I finished showering and walked into the bedroom where Diva was still laying in the same spot on the bed. The only thing that had changed was that she was now naked. When she saw me. She opened her legs and put two fingers inside that tight pink paradise. She gave me a seductive look and said, "Momma needs some attention!" I returned the favor she had so graciously bestowed upon me earlier. As I looked from between her thighs to her eyes, we were both in Heaven. But on my mind all I was thinking was that I had to holla at my nigga.

…

I walked inside the spot. Pat had opened the door and let me in. When I came in the whole house was clouded with smoke. Pat wore a wife beater and shorts. His hair was in a fresh bald fade and a piece and chain sparkled from his neck. He walked back and sat in front of a video game. "Pat" I say.

"Infamous," he responded, not even looking away from the game.

"Damn nigga you too elevated in yo new game to fuck with old faithful friends," I say. Finally, Pat looks up and catches my eye for two beats and then turn back to the video game.

"What you mean," He asks, like he didn't give a fuck.

"You don't even hit a nigga on his line and when I call you to put you on some money you decline," I share and watch as he ½ listens to me.

"I'm trying to see what this herbal shit do. You gotta a potna in crime to assist your grind. You don't need me," he says, confirming my fears. I tried to detect something in his voice, something to indicate the jealously that everybody is trying to convince me that he is now feeling, but his words can't be denied. It felt like he wanted me to choose.

"What you mean nigga you my day one nigga," I yell, frustrated at his nonchalance at the seriousness of the convo. Still I wonder what the fuck this nigga going through? I sat down on his couch and studied him without saying a word. After a minute or so with no reply I break through the silence.

"You don't even fuck with Kristi no more. She been asking about you," I say changing the subject. He made a sucking sound with his teeth and paused the game.

"You trippin nigga ain't nothing changed," He says looking me directly in the eye. We study each other for a minute. I feel a little tingling in my gut.

"I'm trying to do this lightweight shit, get clientele for that and lay low for a minute. Enjoy life!

"Enjoy life? I frown at Pat,"Nigga, what books you been reading," I joke.

"Yeah enjoy life nigga," Pat reiterates, scowling at me.

"What? A nigga don't suppose to enjoy life because he fucking with the streets," I posit. But looking at Pat, this

96

nigga is serious. This ain't the Pat I know or am use to. I look at him for a long moment. I never heard the nigga talk like this. Is this nigga having a midlife crisis or something I wonder. I change my approach.

"Enjoy life nigga I'm just flying to check on my nigga," I say looking at him. He don't even look up maybe there is some truth to what Red, Champagne, and Diva's been saying. I'm glad I heard from the horse's mouth though.

"I'm gone throw this party at my crib next Friday. Diva gonna have some stripper hoes pull up. So show up," I say, inviting him to a different kind of party. He looks at me pointedly.

"What time?"

"It probably won't start until about 10," I confirm.

"I'll pull up and see what it do," he says accepting. It felt like a dismissal though, so I stood up from the couch. I realized it was really nothing else to talk about. I had just got a glimpse into this nigga's heart and I didn't like what I saw.

…

I was sitting on the couch counting money. Diva had pulled off a credit card scam. With the stuff she had bought we had resold for a decent profit. Anything was a decent profit if you hadn't spent nothing. She had bought me a Tank Louis Carfier watch with an alligator band and some gator shoes to match. Diva was about to have me looking like a pimp. I'm not mad though. I called myself a mack anyway. When you live the part you have to look the part.

"Is Red and Champagne coming through today," I call out. Diva entered the living room wearing the purple pantsuit she had worn earlier in the day. She looked like a young, sexy business woman. Her hair was in a straight asymmetrical bob and framing her face.

"They got something set up at a car lot," Diva said, sitting down beside me on the couch and curling her feet up under her.

"Red said that the way it's goin' down, we'll be able to hit for 2 brand-new Bent's," I looked over at Diva excited. We had stepped our game up. We just wasn't hitting ordinary hood licks anymore. Now we were fucking with business credit cards, hitting car lots and stealing safes. We were on some Ocean-Eleven shit like they do in the movies.

"How we gone make that happen? I asked curiously.

"Champagne got something set up with the owner of the lot. He got some type of insurance scam he gone profit," Diva explained. I would have to call Smokey in on this one. Since Da Lot had been off limits, the desire to fuck with any cars had been small. But with 3 brand-new Benzes off the lot, that was a come up that you couldn't pass up. You talking 'bout some big boy shit.

"About what time do they suppose to be here?" Diva asks.

"Probably after 10" I say, finishing counting up the money. We was on some next level shit with this hustling we were doing. We had stepped our game up. Thinking about that made me think about how our fame and hustle has elevated and Pat's had been stagnated. He was now only a low-level drug dealer. That was by choice. He had only been able to purchase himself a second-hand slab. I was ready to come off the lot 3 times. Then let Diva do the same. The game been good to us. After counting the money up, I took it to the bedroom safe and put it up. Me and Diva was making plans to open our own beauty and barbershop. Might as well start investing our money; make our money make more money. A nigga was trying to create some longevity in this shit.

I heard Diva go into the bathroom. After a couple of minutes I heard the shower come on. By the way I could hear it, I knew she had left the bathroom door open. A sign that she wanted some shower loving. She would have to get a rain check on that. I had money on my mind and I was focused on tripling and quadrupling my money. We was really putting our hustle down and the days for hustling backwards was over.

"Smokey" I said into the phone.

"What's the word Mr. Big shot?"

"Money, money and mo' money!" I say, hearing Smokey snicker on the other end.

"That's my language," he said.

"Can you do something with 3 brand-new baby Benz's off the lot?" I ask.

"Can a squirrel do something with acorns and nuts!!" Now it was my time to laugh.

"In the next couple of days I'm gonna be pulling up on you with a star you feel me," I say.

"For 3 with the dealer tags, I'll give you 250 a piece," Smokey says. I did the math. We would have to give the owner a little bit of nothing. I know Red and Champagne got him under their spell. They have too far him to be lifting them make a play for 3 brand-new cars.

"I think they'll go that!"

"Oh I forgot you got you brand-new form!" Smokey said.

"I'm fucking 'with 3 down ass bitches" I say.

"And one of em you fucking!!" Smokey said, speaking truth. I really did not like the way that sounded.

"Yea Diva, that's my #1!" I confirm. We were more than just shacking fuck buddies. She was an extension of me like another limb or an organ. You know when God put Adam to sleep and took that rib out of him. Diva's my rib. After securing the deal with Smokey, Diva was coming out of the bathroom with nothing but a towel on. We locked eyes and as she sashayed off to the bedroom I started to rise. I watched as her hips swished and her ass bounced naked

under the towel she wore. When I was ready, I had enough
time to serve her hard and fast before Champagne and Red
got there. We put in work before and after.

...

"What's up trick?" Red yelled to Diva coming into the front
door
and Champagne was dressed alive in matching tennis skirts
and halter tops their thick thighs was shining as if freshly
oiled.
"What you two hoes doing?" Diva said leading them into
the kitchen. That was the regular spot that they
congregated. I knew that Diva would be
making them a drink. they would gossip for a little while
then they would get to the business. If a dude wanted to
really know what was going on in the streets. All the he had
to do was sit back around a bunch of females and just listen.
They would talk about everything that was going on. Who
was doing who was getting money. Who had beef who was
fronting. all you had to do was shut up and listen.
"Girl P.A. and Lil' 50 ray Pat been talking down on
Infamous," I heard Red try an whisper.
"They say Infamous done got too good for the hood!"
"Bullshit" Diva defended "when did y'all get into this shit?"
"I gave Lil' 50 some pussy to work. The fool start babbling'
on some pillow talk shit" Champagne explained.
"He says the nigga at sounding real bitter." I listened from
the front room. I don't think Pat or Lil 50 so would do any
licking trying to divide or start any bull shit beef between
Pat and me. May be that's why neither one of them came
and told me anything directly. It was kind of band for me to
wrap my brain around anything sour with Pat and me. I I
still wanted to believe we was like twin brothers from
different mothers. I didn't want that to change What did I
do to that nigga. It was Diva that chase me of course I felt
100

the same way for her that she felt for me.

But it wasn't my fault that she didn't cut for Pat. In the beginning we could have shared her.

"Why would be bitter? I heard Diva ask.

"May be the nigga gay and wanted Infamous for himself and now he all about you!" I almost choked on the smoke I had just inhaled gay! Man, Red is crazy Pat wasn't gay.

"Girl you stupid"

"Niggas are weird, bitch," Champagne added. They all looked at me when I entered the kitchen a couple of minutes later. I know they were wondering if I had heard what they were talking about.

"What's up on the come up? "I asked putting everybody mind on the money.

"It goes down tomorrow night at 5," Red answered

"We already got the details worked out." Diva said, looking around at all of us.

"The dude that owns the lot is name Lemont Harper. He's a Jewish asshole whose trying in to squeeze a couple of thousand out of his insurance company! I listened as she explained Lemont and his game. I really didn't give a fuck about his reason for letting us get off with the cars. I just wanted the cars. The cars and the get away.

"We gone pull up like we gone purchase the cars. He's gonna let us supposedly" test drive the vehicles and that's when we do what we do," Champagne added all excited.

"He say if this works out, he'll have more work for us," Red says.

"I think he on some get back shit with all his insurance companies! I really didn't care about Lemont and his issues. You just deal with one lick at a time; completed the first one then moved on to the next one." Champagne finished.

Diva came and stood in front of me. She leaned in with her

arms up and pushed against me close enough to feel my manhood. She kissed me softly and searched my eyes. I knew what she was searching for, too bad she wouldn't find it. My mind was on business only.

Chapter 15

"If it don't make dollars then it don't make sense!" I say. I live and die by that. I was on my way to go see P.A. and Lil 50 since Red and Champagne said that the fools was saying Pat was talking reckless. I wanted to go see what the deal was. Hear what they would tell me if anything.

"Many men wish death up me. Lord I don't cry no mo' don't even look to the sky no mo..." I sung along with 50 Cent blaring from the speakers. My foot heavy on the gas of the new fire Red mustang I was pushing. You could smell the new leather and the tint was darker than a Presidential limo.

"Big shot!" Lil 50 called smiling as I got out of the car. He and P.A. as always was on the block posted like a mailbox.

"Y'all the niggas with the best hand!" I respond, giving P.A. and Lil 50 dap.

"You the one in brand-new tires," P.A. says admiring my car. "That's just a little something minor, I say downplaying my stuntin.'

"Everybody can't move like you" Lil 50 added. "You got you a bad bitch with bad get money potna's. Niggas pray for your position!"

I laughed out loud. He was right, I was doing good. On top

of my game, I came up out of the county all about my mail. I stuck to the plan. Now, I was seeing the benefits from my hard work and dedication.

"What you niggas been on? I asked taking 8-seat on the hood of my car. Lil 50 and P.A. learned against the car. It didn't look like they were starving.

"Bleeding this block 2nd squeezing these hoes for everything they worth Lil 50 responded. He was dressed like he was just off trip to the mall. P.A. looked like he had been on the block the last two days.

"You niggas hustle the mud for moistness and the dirt for grit."

"We still in the trenches. Everybody ain't fit to fuck around white collar shit. So you gotta play your position and let others play theirs." P.A. says.

"We ain't mad at Ya!" Lil 50 began and I heard the emphasis he put on we.

"Rise like yeast and bake yo cakes. Just don't forget to chunk yo real potnas a slice of sweetness every once in a while." He finished. I looked at P.A. and Lil 50 suspiciously. Was he trying to tell me something.

"When was the last time you fucked with Pat?" P.A. said. There it go! I knew something was up.

"He been trying to fuck with that weed shit," I responded looking from P.A. to Lil' 50.

"You ain't put him on no licks?" P.A asked. His face betraying nothing.

"Man every time I ask that nigga if he want to link up with me and Diva on some bread he don't want to fuck around!" I say.

"That's yo' day one nigga ain't it? P.A. asks. I frown at him.

"What kind of question is that?" I respond as P.A. and Lil 50 exchange a look.

"Y'all don't seem to be so tight like y'all use to be" Lil 50 said stating the obvious.

"That's still my nigga. He just got his agenda and I got mine," I say as they exchange an even more telling look. "Why?" I ask trying to get answers. "Y'all done heard something I haven't?" There goes that look again. I study at both of them closely. Trying to read what they ain't saying.

"You and that nigga use to be like conjoined twins when that nigga ate you shit" Lil 50 said looking at me intently. "Y'all use to be on some grimey shit!'

"Like I say. Our hustles just differ now. He want to do some other shit. That's still my nigga" P.A. and Lil 50 shared a look, now a bit more suspicious than before. What the fuck? "Stay on yo' toes daddy Judas betrayed Jesus and he was one of the 12!!!" Lil' 50 warned. They put me on high alert.

…

"Why niggas soft when it come to pussy? Red asked laying naked in Champagne's arms. The room smelt like kush, sex, and sweat.

"They'll turn on their own flesh and blood, huh?" Champagne asked rhetorically. She caressed Red's soft skin. Although Red acted so hard she was literally soft as cotton.

"You know Pat probably already had some hatred for Infamous even before Diva!" Red said looking deeply into the situation.

"Neither one of them at really knew Diva before the other so what right do Pat have to feel some type of way about anything.

"Diva!" Champagne thought about what Red just had said about Pat probably already had a hidden hatred for Infamous as she hugged Red close."

"You know it'll always be us against the world right?' Red said, looking up at Champagne with naked trust in her eyes.

"Until the world blow Red!!" Champagne responded. She inclined her head to Red and met her with the deepest sweetest kiss. They kissed deeply as her hand slid inside Red. As their lips locked, Red's eyes closed, both of them moaning deeply as tongues wagged in each of their throats and in and around their mouths in ecstasy.

"No nigga, no bitch!" they said in unison, when they came up for air. Their bond was unshakeable.

"Do you think that Diva and Infamous. Make a good duo." Red asked.

"I think they fit." Champagne responded after a pregnant pause.

"By fit, you mean the one compliments and completes the other."

"Exactly" Champagne confirmed. "Diva and Infamous met and just clicked."

Red and Champagne liked that their friend had found somebody she was equal with and

that actually gave a damn about her as a person not just her and her body, But now his so-called "Day one nigga" was bitter and acting up.

"I think Pat gone jump on some shady shit. That nigga movements got to be monitored!!" Red pronounced.

Chapter 16

"I think I'm Big Meech-, Larry Hoover, Whippin' work, Hallelujah. One nation under God-Real niggas getting' money from the fucking start..." Rick Ross bumped hard from the surround sound while his music video played from the large flat screen.

"Money is the motive, hater-hurting is the inspiration," I said, taking a sip of the rum and Coke. It was a party, but I had a small audience on the apartment balcony P.A. Lil 50 and a few of the other hood homies was chill-laxing and celebrating the prosperity. We had several blunts circulating and was in our zone.

"You gotta become a mover and shaker in this game," I was on my level and feeling myself. So far everything I was touching was turning into gold. Every lick equaled major profit. Things just felt different. I was feeling that my hustle had elevated to a high state. I was
 same big boy shit.

"Be true to the game and the game will true to you!" P.A. added.

"Get shady and you gone see a bunch of dark days! Lil 50 said.

"The game got a God and he will punish you severely for

any violations!" I lifted my cup up at what Lil 50 stated.

"I'll toast to that!" I say, cosigning.

"You niggas act like y'all in the movies" Don Don joked. "All of this Tony Montana dialogue," Everybody in the room laughed. It may have sounded cinematic to the average low level game mind. But what was being spoken was some true to life shit. Be true to the game and it shall be true to you! In life you reap what you sew! I looked out at the clear night. The downtown city lights of Houston Texas twinkled, blinked, and glowed in the distance from the second-floor balcony. I had started off and had been pushing for peanuts. I was moving on a small scale and had really thought I had been on some "Big Dog" shit. I was eating puppy chow and thought I had been tasting kibbles? Bits now that I had felt the inside of genuine silk, polyester just wouldn't do!

"Hey daddy, you good!?" Diva asked sweetly as she came out to the balcony with a drink for me.

"Yeah, momma, what's good!? I responded grabbing the drink and pulling her into me for a quick embrace. She was wearing a jersey dress emphasizing all her curves and complimenting her sculpted thighs and well-defined calves. I watched the lust and envy in niggas eyes as she twisted off.

"You got you a thoroughbred for real," Lil 50 said shifting his eyes off Diva's swaying hips and thick ass towards me. We had all been watching her walk away. It was some strange shit but every time I was looking at Diva it's like I was seeing her for the very first time. I was still infatuated with her even though we was deep into this thing by now.

"Yeah that's my shawty for real" I said insistently.

"Bitches bring envy to a nigga door step without even trying!" P.A. said, fucking up the moment.

"Bad bitches anyway!" added Lil 50.

108

"Why would niggas envy when the world is full of bad bitches," I said, feeling some type of way about this routine of them suggesting I had a lot of haters.

"Bad bitches come a dime a dozen cuz!" Slicky said. He was a tall lanky ass dude with straight cornrows. He was a old Snoop Dogg looking nigga but with build. He was a scrawny version of Kawhi Leonar, the NBA player.

"The baddest bitches are tailormade for the Bossest niggas." He continued.

"Every nigga can't handle no bad bitch. Their mind ain't strong enough." Everyone was listening including me. I was always a sponge for top notch game.

"A bad body don't make a bad bitch! If she can't think and all she can do is look fly. You might as well get you a mannequin!"

"True dat," P.A. agreed as Slicky's hood philosophy lesson continued. I just smiled. I had me the authentic bad bitch according to the definition that Slicky gave. All of a sudden I felt tension in the air. I frowned and began to look around and lo and behold, standing at the door that led out to the balcony was Pat. At first I thought I saw a look of raw hatred if it was it was only there for a couple of seconds. Then we locked eyes and Pat smiled.

"Infamous!"

"Pat" I responded hesitantly but matching his enthusiasm. He walked around and greeted everyone, then he pulled me in for that one arm bro hug.

"Infamous da Almighty!" He said smiling I smiled back.

"Pat the Herbal magician." I said mocking his new venture as he pulled a zip lock bag of the from his baggy Jeans.

"Right on, right on!" Pat said laughing.

"You boys need to get on this," he said as he pulled a couple of sweets from his pocket.

"This some Jamican Rastafarian, I'll lull yo ass to sleep type shit!" Everyone laughed and inched forward anticipating the mellow as high weed gives.

"Come on Infamous you gotta do the honors," Pat held the sack and a couple of sweets out to me. I took the offered material and went to roll the fastest blunt I could. We lit it up and smoked hard. After everybody had sampled the exotic herb. I was on some 'Super Me'-type shit.

"What's good Pat? You don't even come around no more!" I said, watching his eyes.

"Nigga I just been ducked off listening to the stories of your rise to prominence!" Pat responded. I tried to detect any sour emotion in his voice.

"You supposed to be right here with a nigga!" I told him getting serious. He looked off. Everything just seemed to get quiet. Everybody had pretty much drifted off back into the party. The smoke had them festive. Diva had come to the door and saw me and Pat alone talking. She looked at me with a question. I nodded and she drifted back off into the background. I know she was somewhere close watching and ready if something needed to pop off.

"We got different paths next Infamous. Different ambitions. We on two different levels," Pat said.

"Nigga listen to yourself," I said, trying to snap him out of his bullshit explanation for abandoning a nigga. Even though I would never admit it, what this nigga was saying was hurting. I loved this nigga like a brother. We grew up together from the dirt. Fight and fucking together.

"Nigga we two niggas from the same kind. I think with your mind!" I say trying to connect.

Pat's blank look said it all. He stared into my eyes for a second, and with no words to respond to my soliloquy, he looked off.

"Shit change, cuz and people do too!" Pat responded, moving towards the door. P.A. and Lil 50 were right.

110

"I just wanted to came thru to show face. See haw you and yo fam was doing!" he said before stopping at the door. He looked back at me as of to say goodbye, but again, no words.

"You and Diva doing y'all best shit." He added, looking me deep in the eyes.

"You beat me to her…" He said reluctantly. He looked like he wanted to say more but he just turned and walked into the apartment. I watched him disappear. After a couple of minutes of being lost in deep thought. Diva came out and snapped me out of my feelings with her sexy ass hip switching, a drink and her sassy mouth.

"You should've shot 'em," she said as she passed me the drink.

…

"What y'all niggas want all y'all niggas need…" Eve of Ruff Ryders was rapping from the speakers. Champagne was sitting in the passenger seat of the white Toyota Camry. In her lap was a nickel plated 45 right beside a mirror covered in white powder.

"What's yo infatuation with pussy!" Pat asked. He was driving down 288.

"I don't have infatuation with pussy! I got love for women! Something you niggas will never understand!" she responded. Champagne and Pat had been silently creeping for a couple of weeks now behind Red's back. He had run into her of all places at a grocery store. He had been out just enjoying the day while he was anticipating a call from his connect so he could re-up. He had moved from trapping to mapping! He was high and had gotten the munchies. Too impatient and hungry to drive to the next fast food place, he stopped off at the small store. He had run into Champagne in the snack aisle. They started off in a cordial conversation. Then next.

"It's the same thang ain't it?" Pat responded.

"Naw, it's not the same nigga!" Champagne retorted as Pat gave her a confused look.

"What's the difference? He asked wanting to know. Champagne looked at him for a couple of seconds.

"I'm infatuated with a woman's emotions, her chemistry, the softness. It's more than the wetness between her legs." Pat listened to Champagne intently. He hadn't yet recognized her female energy while she talked but soon her would.

"With you dudes, y'all objectify everything. Y'all try to possess when a female's natural instinct is passion."

"Whatever!" Pat responded, Champagne rolled her eyes. She snorted a long line off the mirror and passed it under Pat's nose so he could get his head right as he drove.

"Anyway, I know you will hit on this side of the diamond so that's what matters" Champagne looked upside Pat's head not liking the way he worded his last statement.

"I know love doesn't exist!" Pat continued. "Lust prevails while, love fails!" he quoted.

"Where all this muthafuckin' conversation about love come from?" Champagne asks with a scowl. Here this nigga is with this soft shit she thought.

"I'm just saying!" Pat shot back.

"Nigga the first law of nature is self-preservation, so this shit speaks for itself" Champagne looked at Pat. How have this nigga survived so long being so soft. She had been on to the sexual chemistry that her and Pat shared. They had hit a couple licks together. But their relationship was mostly sexual as she was in-love with Red. That had been her girl for like 6 years now. But Champagne still needed to feel that man's touch. That male energy and penile erection inside of her for full satisfaction. She chose

Pat, thinking he was the safest bet. She could satisfy those urges with him and not worry about neither one of them getting attached and tripping. Red was hers for life Red was wifey. But Pat was just dick.

"What's going on with you feelings with you day one nigga Infamous? Champagne asked. Pat looked over at her surprised. His eyes squinting, curious what she was getting at.

"What you mean 'feeling's with Infamous?'"

"Nigga you know what I mean!" Champagne pressed. Pat stared straight ahead as if he didn't hear her. Champagne waited him out, watching him closely. He remained quiet for three long minutes. He glanced over at her. She saw a mask com over his face.

"That nigga really sold me out!" Pat finally admitted. Champagne hid her grimace.

"How did he do that?" she asked, trying to get him to say more.

"He knew I wanted Diva but he made her his main gal!" Champagne studied Pats face. This nigga was serious from the looks of it. He still had it bad and was still feeling some type of way about everything.

"You for real?" Champagne asked in disbelief, but already knowing the answer.

"Me and that nigga use to be like arms and legs connected to one body. We moved on one accord, Now…" Pat continued his speech as Champagne stop listening as she thought to herself, 'Damn this nigga has to be softer than melted butter.'

"Did you at anytime tell 'I' how you was feeling," Champagne asked.

"I don't have to that nigga know what he was doing. He know how I felt."

"How you know he knew. Did he tell you that?" Pat

113

frowned over at Champagne's response.

"What the fuck is this? Question and answering session!!" Pat sulked, trying to shift the pressure.

"Nigga get out yo feelings, I'm just trying to find out why you and yo potna ain't potna's no more." Champagne pushed back. Giving Pat a dirty look.

"When we first cut into ya'll, you and that nigga used to complete each other sentences, now y'all very seldom even speak to each other." Champagne retorted.

"Man, fuck Infamous, I'm doing what I do and he doing what he do!" Pat said angrily settling the argument. Champagne looked into himand saw bitterness that seeped hrough the mask

that Pat had tried to put on. Champagne knew then that Pat was dangerous.

...

"Nigga you move one more stutter step I'll pump this lead in yo' ass so fast..." Infamous warned was pointing the big 45 rugger at the check cashing place employee. The employee had come out to make a food run for he and his co-workers something that he did regularly. Today I was waiting. The tall pink-faced young white boy paused at first sight, frightened with the door open. I pushed him back inside. The gun pointed at his temple.

"Anybody feeling heroic, then we gone need somebody to pray for this white boy's soul." I looked around at all the employees. It was only three, not including the white guy I held

at gun point. They all just stared at me with fear in their eyes. The shit would have looked comical if this wasn't to real live shit. But my wildly beating heart reassured me that this was the actual factual.

"What the fuck is ya'll standing staring for. Y'all know what the business is! I barked at a young pimply-faced

114

white girl to move first towards the cash drawer. My eyes roamed the room. Any sudden moves then I was catching a body. I was on this one by myself. Diva was somewhere abusing somebody's credit cards instead of sitting idle. I had decided to come on this caper solo. It had already been planned in advance not for the particular night. But set up.

"Give me what I need and I'll be on my way!" I coached. "Now I want all y'all to get in a line like we on Soul Train. We gone work our way to the A/V room," I said. With the surveillance tapes, any funny business all y'all gone embrace an early death!"

After securing the tapes, I got the fuck out of dodge. I was sweating up under the cloth mask I wore that only left a part of my eyes showing. I quickly jumped in the small sports car I had stolen for this lick and rolled calmly out of the parking lot. I wasn't even ½ a block away when the first police car sped passed me, lights flashing and sirens blaring. As soon as I was safe distance away I put more weight on my foot and pushed quickly out of the area. When I made it to our apartment, it was a million shopping bags littering the living room, Diva

was off again. Still putting in more work. Tonight will be a super prosperous night. I went straight to the bedroom. Throwing the bag of bills on the bed, I quickly stripped out of all my clothes and jumped into a cold shower and washed for damn near an hour. My skin was wrinkled like I was over 90 years old. I came out the bathroom and ran into Diva and Red.

"Boy!" Diva yelled. I saw as Red eyes quickly traveled down to my large penis. She then looked me in the eyes and looked off.

"Put some clothes on! I slowly walked to the dresser drawer and pulled out a fresh pair of crisp boxers. Diva had took to ironing my boxers with my clothes. It was a funny feeling to feel the starched cloth on my nuts and ass.

"Why you walking' around the house showing my shit off while I got company?" Diva griped.

"First off, this is my house and I can walk around this muthafucker any way I feel like it," I shot back.

"Secondly, I didn't know we had company!" Diva rolled her eyes. Her and Red was going through the sacks of merchandise they had accumulated from their hustle.

"Well now that you do know you need to put some clothes on!" Diva was feeling feisty. I stared at her for a long moment. She looked back defiantly before cracking a smile.

"Don't start showing out cause you got company!!" I warned. I couldn't let her step too out of bounds especially in front of company.

"Ain't nobody showing 'out' I 'm just trying to make YOU stop showing 'off!" She replied snidely. I gave her a look that made her silent. Then I finished putting on my clothes.

"Look, we ain't gone even start playing those games!" I didn't have to explain myself further.

"We got like 16 to 17 thousand dollars worth of shit!" Diva said changing the subject. I looked over all the bags that cluttered the bedroom.

They had dresses, purses and boxes of perfume scattered across the bed. They had boxes of fancy shoes too.

"I see y'all had a pretty productive day!"

"Nigga we had more than a productive day. We did the damn thang!" Red exclaimed.

"Yea, we did do our best shit!" Diva agreed. They both laughed and gave each other a high fives. I looked from one to the other. Diva's chocolate skin was glowing along with her eyes. Diva was excited and thrilled after her day of success. Red was looking like she did this every day.

"I hit that check cashing place." I informed Diva. She looked up at me.

"I felt like I could handle that shit one deep. So, I went in!" Her and Red exchanged looks.

"Tell me you lyin'" Diva said with a look of concern. I looked at her disappointed at her reaction.

"Fuck, I'm gonna lie about shit like that for!"

"That was real stupid Infamous!" Diva scolded.

"In what way?"

"You know we had that shit planned out perfectly." Diva responded.

"What if you would've got popped?" She was right, but I didn't like her suggestion.

"Well, I didn't !" I went and got the sack with all the money. I dumped all the 20s, 50s and 100-dollar bills on the bed on top of the other stuff they had spread out. The money would only have to be split two ways. But I knew Diva would share some of her money with Red and Champagne. That's what she always did. I estimated between 10 to 12 stacks that I

pulled from the checking place. A good 1-man lick. I was about ready to start trying to clean my money. Me and Diva had been stacking money. We was planning to open a beauty and

barber shop. We had discussed buying a house. We were tired of the renting. Plus we had been trying to go ½ on a baby, so far we had been short some change.

"This nigga crazy!" Diva said to Red, shaking her head as she grabbed the money I handed her. A little pocket change. A little later after all the money was counted the merchandise separated split, we had a few spots to get rid of some of the clothes and shoes. We were sitting in the living room sharing a blunt. Diva was laid with her head in

my lap. Champagne had shown up a few
minutes before. She and Red was sitting on the floor. They had some uno
cards and they acted like a grade-school girls with the giggles every other minute. Rubbing
Divas forehead and looking into her eyes, I asked:
"Are you really into a nigga like you seem to be or are you just playing yo' role?" She glared at me in disapproval.
"Nigga what kind of question is that?"
"Are you?"
"Stop playin with me Infamous!" She responded losing all her cool. I looked at her for a long while. Red and Champagne were looking intently. We smiled to break the tension.
"Shit about to get real and I need to know that you're on deck for the duration," I began.
"We' bout to step into a whole zone that's next level. Loyalties are about to be tested. Money does that!" I preached. Diva just listened to me talk. I saw in her eyes then, trust, sincerity and loyalty. But how long will that last. Money always tends to corrupt peoples mind, morals and integrity the more they gain the more they want. The more they have the greedier they become. It's a weird thing with people and power. Money brings power. The more money the
more power. After being powerless for so long, some people don't know how to handle power.
"Nigga, I came from nothing. But nothing material makes me. I give value to material things. Not the other way around." Diva responded.
"What is this? An episode of 'money, power and the streets?" Red cut in from the floor.
"Mind yo business?" I said giving her a look. Me and Diva looked at each other for a long minute. We both searching

for an answer or reassurance that we would not find in each other eyes. Only time will reveal future actions.

"All I know how to do is be real. The only thing changes with me is my fashion! "Diva spoke. I heard smacking sounds and looked down and Champagne and Red was going at it. Looking like they were trying to suck the skin off each others lips. I don't know what part of our conversation got them so sexually wired. But I watched them for a minute with their hands and arms squeezing and fingering each other's body parts. Then I looked down at Diva. Her eyes were twinkling with mischievousness. Hearing the moans turned her on. Then I got excited. As my penis started to rise,

I looked down and saw Red had Champagne's jeans and panties down to her ankles and was working her hands and tongue between her legs while Champagne's legs spread eagle, with her back arched, and eyes closed tightly whimpering from the pleasure. Damn, Champagne's moans was making it really hard for me. Diva was now sitting up also watching the show, while she rubbed my member. I reached over and started massaging Diva's firm breasts, her nipples already hard, begged for my attention. I put my mouth on her breast through her shirt. Biting and nipping at the thin material covering her chest, then I ripped her shirt off. All types of erotic sounds could be heard coming from my living room. We watched Red and Champagne maneuver to the 69 position and focus on pleasing each other. Getting overly excited, me and Diva got into the act. From her neck to waist, I nibbled, kissed, and bit. I went to the wetness between her legs and mimicked what I watched Red do to get Champagne off. Before long, Diva's chocolate thighs was squeezing my face and she was screaming in pleasure like never before. I guess you can learn a lot from two women pleasing each other. Red and Champagne was caught up in the excitement too. It's like we all were competing to see who could scream the loudest and cum the hardest. I was harder than reinforced steel. I pushed hard and quick into Diva as her body started trembling. Her manicured nails dug into my back. I had caught her just as she coming from my licking and there was no stopping me after that warm, wet, vibrating feeling from her body.

"Damn girl you super tight!" I moaned. I could feel her wetness on my balls. I pumped in and out of her. I slowed my pace and rhythm to try and make it last a little longer.

"This is my pussy!" I said as I long stroked and went deep. Fucking Diva just the way she liked it.

"Ooooohhhh nigggaaa," she moaned pulling me into her

"You love this dick don't ya!" I shot back.

"Ggiivve iiittt too meee!" she said as she started bucking up, to meet my thrusts. I didn't wanna stop our bodies synchronized undulations.

"Uuuhh shit! I wrapped my hands around her neck.

"DDDaaadddyyy!" I stroked her and choked her until we both orgasmed. Panting and trying to catch my breath. I laid down on top of her. All of a sudden, we were back in reality. Red and Champagne started clapping. Too weak to do anything, I rolled off Diva and just laid beside her on the couch.

"Girl he almost fucked you to death literally," Red said, laying naked beside Champagne on the floor.

"Y'all some freaky kinky muthafuckers" Champagne added.

"Don't get no ideas' bitch!" Diva said half-jokingly.

120

Chapter 17

"I would like to open savings account." I was in Wells Fargo Bank in a suit and tie. I felt really professional. I had bought me a 3-piece suit at Men's Warehouse. Instead of alligators, I bought some Stacy Adams shoes. I threw on some wire rimmed glasses to complete the sophisticated look. A pale-skinned skinny white chick with blonde hair that hung to the middle of her back asked me for an assortment of information.

"Have you ever banked here before sir,? She asked in sultry southern drawl.

"No mam!" she looked me over as if reappraising me.

"You know you have to put" 50 or more to start a savings account?"

"I brought $700" I responded pulling 100-dollar bills from the wallet I bought only for this occasion.

"You can also sign up for direct deposit," she said, pitching to get that extra commission. I was here today for one purpose only. That was to lay down the foundation for our transition. At first, I started to do a joint account with me and Diva, but decided against it. Although we were strong now, today was established already but tomorrow was unknown and uncertain.

"All I want is a saving account right now." I said politely. "Just fill out these forms" she said handing me a semi-thick stack of forms. Damn, all this just to place money in an account.

"If you have any questions just get my attention," she left for the next customer walking in as I looked through all the seemingly unnecessary paperwork. Well, a nigga gotta begin somewhere!!

...

"This looks like a good spot to open a shop" I said, pulling to a stop in the parking lot of the small strip mall. They had a retail store, a credit union and a cricket wireless. In between the
credit union and the retail store was a small space with a 'for lease' sign hanging in the window.

"It is a good spot for a beauty shop," Diva agreed looking around. We got out the car, looking through the floor-to-ceiling glass windows. I had Diva call the number that was on the sign. She called and set up a viewing with the realtor. We weren't looking for too big of a space. Just someplace to help us wash our money.

"Y'all done started breaking into buildings. I looked back at the sound of the familiar voice. Times gotta be hard!" Pat laughed. He was wearing a throwback jersey and shorts with all white air force ones on his feet. I tried to fix my face. "Naw pimpin B & Es are not our steez. We got effortless ways to make G's!" I responded. He looked at Diva in her Daisy Dukes and ½ top you could see the naked lust in Pat's
eyes.

"We really don't have to hit another lick. All we really have to do is watch our money make money!" Diva popped off. Pat looked at Diva his eyes clouding for a minute.

"What's good with you nigga?" I pulled Pat's attention to

122

me. It took him a couple of seconds but he finally looked at me.

"Keeping my 10 toes flat, making sure my paper stack. Cause money has always been the motive!" He responded.

"Yeah it has," I said plainly, not really knowing what Pat was trying to insinuate. He looked back over at Diva then at me.

"Damn, Infamous you must be getting 'T' at the 'D' Because the longest I ever seen you keep a bitch around was for 48 hrs!!" Okay now this nigga was tripping. I glanced over at Diva, she was just watching Pat closely not saying nothing with a straight face. A quiet Diva was a dangerous Diva.

"The only tender things I fuck with is steaks and hams!" I shot back. Here this nigga go
 showing his hate.

"And the reason why Diva is around is because she not your average bitch. Her name speaks
 for itself'" I said defending her honor.

"Damn cuz is that heat I detect under that cool exterior you dressed in?" Pat asked feeling the energy coming off my body. I mean this use to be my every day all day nigga. Now he was on some playground "You kissed the girl I dreamed of all my life" type shit.

"I'm cool but it seems like you got some juice on yo chest!" We locked heated eyes. He staring me down while I did the same. Neither of us intimidated but only one of us feeling any type of hatred. If anything I was disappointed and hurt. I had a unique type of brotherly
 love for Pat! And here this nigga was sour with me because Diva chose me and I chose her. All our feelings were mutual nothing about our hook up was slick or shady.

"Man, fuck this shit!?" Diva broke into our silent mental battle.

"Pat I was not feeling' you like that. It was I who had my

eye from the start up. you didn't ever have nothing coming. So stop acting like 'I' short stopped you on my pussy!" she was heated and ghetto fabulous. Her microbraids swinging with each roll of her neck. She looked
so fucking sexy when she was mad. But this was some real shit. Pat burst into laughter all of sudden.
"Bitch, get out yo' ego. This ain't even about you!" Pat lied.
"This shit deeper than your uterus!" I tensed up at the disrespect he was swinging at Diva. This nigga was gonna make me take this shit to a dark space."
"Watch the disrespect you toss at my lil momma!" I warned. My voice underlining the threat. Pat locked eyes with me and we belted mentally.
"I'm glad you exposed 'your' true colors now rather than later," Pat said. Diva came in between us trying to chill the heat that was quickly rising.
"Pat you need to grow the fuck up and accept the facts, nigga step yo swag up. Maybe you can one day obtain a bitch like me!!" Diva grabbed my arm and started nudging me back towards our car.
"Come one daddy, we got moves to make and hater's to shake."

...

"Man I don't know what's wrong with that nigga!" I was over Lil 50 apartment venting about the situation with me and Pat.
"Its like he a whole brand new nigga!" I said. We were in Lil 50's kitchen. He was measuring and cutting cake. He wore a chef's hat and apron like he was really whipping up a meal.
"That nigga clowned out like that?" Lil 50 asked.
"Fucked me up too," I responded with a sigh.
"What's really fuckin me up though is because I don't know how to react towards the nigga!" I shook my head with
124

frustration.

"I can't just hate the nigga like he seem to be hatin' me. I'm too real for that!" I took another

puff of the good sticky and tried to settle my nerves. But the more I spoke on this shit the more I thought about it. The more wired I'd become.

"Shid, why not? The nigga hatin you!" Lil 50 said frowning at me like I was the most stupidest man in the World.

"But if I do the same thing he doing that makes me no better than he is!"

"Right, right!'" Lil 50 nodded his head in agreement.

"After all me and that nigga done faded as one. He get's shady with bright Sun!" My feelings was hurt and I was sounding like a little bitch. I knew it, but couldn't help it. Pat was my brother from another mother.

"What ya lil momma gotta say about all that " 50 asked.

"She tried to tell that nigga! That they never had a chance to begin with," I responded shaking my head.

"But that don't matter because that nigga pride hurt and his ego is riddled with bullet holes!" Lil 50 laughed at my analogy. He began packaging little small packs of coke. He was getting ready to flood a block or two.

"Keep doing you pimp. Fuck that soft ass nigga." 50 said.

All the homies know that Pat was on some other shit. Everybody felt that he was wrong in the actions he was taking towards me. The attitude he was adopting. I know a lot of people didn't tell Pat that because they were afraid of his wrath. They may have talked that shit in the presence of me. But confronted by Pat himself. Them bastards would try to act more neutral than the gear shift. May be 50 would repeat himself but that's about it. Diva, Champagne and Red would stand their ground.

"I really want to just go ahead and rumble with that nigga. Go with him from the shoulders!" I said looking at 50.

"Maybe he'll come out the victor in that, but I still want to get this frustration with him out of my system," I complained. I was really messed up about this situation nobody really knew what I was going through and I did not know how to really deal with the feelings and emotions I was experiencing.

"This shit is really fucking 'you up huh," Lil 50 worried. "Yeah, really!" Lil 50 chuckled when he looked and seen that I hadn't even cracked a smirk He threw up one hand. "Alright Infamous I feel ya. The only thing you can do is ex that nigga from your circle. If he ever come around with anything sideways. you deal with the nigga violation without mercy. Finally he was getting it. Now he saw or at least got a sense of my anger at Pat. I needed that fool crushed eventually I knew I would have to do it. At first any type of thought of doing any type of harm to Pat would've had me feeling some type of way. Now, I wanted that nigga erased from my memory. I want to forget I ever knew that fool.

We sat in Lil 50' living room. MTV Cribs was on and they were showing this bad ass mansion.

"Could you imagine living in that shit!" I asked looking at Lil 50.He looked up from the sweet he was rolling.

"I'm gone be living in one bigger, 50 said, going back to rolling. I looked at him without saying anything for a couple of seconds and then looked back at the T.V. I believed 50. He was ambitious like that now. It's like overnight all of our ambitions and drives had grown and gotten stronger. Nobody was satisfied with a petty hustle anymore. Nigga was hustling for more than just a car and some clothes.

"I was in Bellaire the other day and I had a vision of me just having a chill out spot there!" I said.

"You got enough bread right now to make that happen,

what you waiting on!" 50 responded.

"First we want to get the beauty shop established. We can't lease the building. And buy all the equipment on skit all at once.

"Nigga the start up for a business is steep!'" I informed 50. We had done all our homework. Researched and did the math and we knew what we had to do to succeed. Success was the goal.

"Sound like you know what you doing and where you headed," 50 said, passing the blunt to me.

"Nigga, it's been a long grind. A nigga ain't been doing all this hustling for nothing." I stated, taking a long drag on the blunt.

"I need you on this other idea I have brewing!" I said getting to point that I had come for any way. 50 looked at me expectantly, so I continued.

"I want to open this butt naked house." I said.

"You know how nigga's is so 'I'm gone need a head bust on deck to keep shit smooth." I finished looking at 50. Not only did Lil 50 have an intimidating look about him. He was about the business too. Plus he already had a slight reputation for playing with pistols. So, I know nigga's will respect his ganxta from the on-set.

"You can pump work up out the house too. That way you don't have to stop or neglect your business to fuck with mine." I said. Lil 50 listened to my pitch. I could see his eyes calculating. His mind working. He was mostly thinking about the pussy he'd be able to get. Money was the motive sure, but cumming would be the cherry topper!

"You got a lot goin' on'" Lil 50 said skeptically. "You want to do a beauty shop and a butt naked house. How that's gone work out?" Lil 50 asked.

"Well we gone do the house sooner. We still working on the permit and shit with the beauty shop. It don't really take too much on the house" I said.

"We already got the ball rolling on that already. I'm gonna be ready on that by next month. You gone be ready! Lil 50 looked at me strangely.

"So you already had this planned?" He asked.

"What do you mean?" I asked not completely understanding what he meant by the question.

"You already knew or thought you knew that I would accept the position you was offering'"

"Naw, playa! With or without you we opening the club up when I thought about security,

you came to mind," I explained. Lil 50 studied me for a minute.

"What is this paying?"

"500 a night. You keep all profits from your business and all the pussy you can handle." I said watching him. I knew he was on board. He would work for free just to be around the females. Lil 50 was a pussy hound.

"When you gone hire your girls? I want to be there for the interview phase. Lil 50 smiled.

"Diva, Red and Champagne got a line up already set up," I responded as Lil 50 laughed.

"I should've known!"

"You oughta get Champagne and Red to get up there and twerk. That whole dike act will pull in so much money. I'm telling you! Lil 50 looked like he was getting excited just thinking about it.

"The grand opening gone be the shit "I said adding to the hype in his mind,

"I'm in cuz!"

Chapter 18

"Fuck me nigga!" Champagne growled. Pat butt naked sweating, jumped in and out of Champagne, his hard pulsing making smacking sounds for the world to hear. "That's all you got nigga!" she challenged as the pain became pleasure. She threw her hips back at him, matching him rhythm for rhythm.

"Own this pussy. Own, own it nigga," she dug her nails into his back. Her skin flush as her breathing becoming choppy. "Awww shi I'm I'm bout to c-c..u.u.u.u.mmmm!" Champagne gripped and pulled at the carpet as her orgasm kept building like waves. She bit into Pat's shoulders and muffled her screams.

"Ahhhhhhh!!!!" Pat grabbed a handful of Champagne hair and pulled as he pushed deep inside her and spilled his hot seed.

"Fu,Fu Fucc fuck !!" Pat breathed collapsing on top of Champagne. Exhausted and out of breath Champagne, laid there breathing heavy shivering. Her eyes were opened and glazed over. Pat rolled off of her.

"Shit," he breathed out and immediately felt asleep.

…

Pat awoke to the feel of Champagne's warm wet mouth on

his rock hard manhood with half-closed eyes. He watched her lips suck and lick at the head of his dick. She looked as if she was locked in a zone. Pat watched her mouth make love to his dick. He reached out and ran his hand through her wild uncombed her. She had that freshly fucked look. As she swallowed Pat whole, she looked seductively in his eyes and moaned deep in her throat.

"Damn!" Pat moaned. He felt the pressure building in his balls. Champagne felt him growing on her tongue. She produced more saliva and let her hands go to work, adding to the pressure. Holding him at the base of his penis she moved her mouth up and down on him with her warm, wet mouth and her soft supple lips. Making greedy wet sounds she rotated her neck and worked her hands until Pat was shooting down her throat. She milked him for every drop of semen he produced, pulling her mouth off of him, her mouth made that popping sound. She smiled and licked her lips.

"I'm that bitch!!" she bragged.

···

Later they were in the shower, washing each other bodies. Pat behind Champagne massaged a skin moisturizer into her back.

"Nigga, we gotta stop this !!" Champagne said all of a sudden. Immediately Pat's hand stopped. He frowned at the back of her slender neck.

"Fuck, wrong with you? Pat asked feeling some type of way.

"This shit ain't right!" Champagne said softly. No shit! All of sudden this bitch done caught a case of consciousness.

"What you mean?" Pat asked.

"Red is my baby and here I am over here with your cum leaking from between my thighs." Pat resumed rubbing her body down.

130

"You don't think Red getting her no dick on the side!" Pat said.

"It don't matter what she is or not doing' The point is I'm being unfaithful," Champagne argued.

"I'm goin' back to her with the feel of your dick on my tongue, telling her I love her," Champagne turned around so she can face Pat.

"I know it ain't shit to you!" she said looking at him.

"But I take my loyalties seriously," Pat burst out laughing which caused Champagne to get mad. What the fuck was so funny.

"You take your loyalties seriously?" Pat echoed her.

"You take your loyalties seriously, but we been fucking and sucking for the last 2 months!" Pat looked Champagne deep in her eyes.

"Come on baby girl, be real. 'bout this shit you only got one loyalty you take seriously. That's yourself!"

"Nigga, you don't know me!" Champagne responded.

"I don't know you" You right. But I click with your character. We two of the same kind.

"Nigga we not the same, we don't click. We fuck!!" Champagne responded. Pat looked at the anger and guilt color her face. What the fuck he was suppose to do feel sorry for her. Tell her she's right. They need to stop doing what they doing. It's wrong.

"We do all that so what's the problem all of a sudden."

"This shit has been consensual. A nigga ain't forced or coerced you into shit!" Champagne eyes narrowed as Pat told the truth.

"You a rotten nigga Pat." She said stepping away from him and out of the shower.

"I can't do this shit no more. I made a mistake. I gotta go!!" Champagne gathered her clothes from the floor. Dropping water everywhere, she was moving quickly, trying to hurry and get the fuck out of dodge.

"So you gone turn your back on a nigga too!" Pat said watching Champagne gather up all her shit.

"All of y'all are meant for each other. You, Red, Diva, Infamous. Ain't none of y'all bout shit!" Pat shot. His eyes burned with hatred. His mind was spinning. He watched her walk out of the bathroom. He knew in a few minutes she would be gone. Although he wasn't in love with Champagne. He did have feelings for her over the short period of their affairs she had made He didn't fall in love, but he did become attached. He had began to feel her vibes.

"All y'all gone get y'alls ! He vowed "you played pussy Infamous, now it's time that you get fucked !!"

Chapter 19

Infamous and Diva finally had the beauty shop up and running. It was called Diva'd Down They had hired several beauticians and nail techs. They were on their way of recouping the money they had put in. Infamous had opened a buttnaked house on the South side. Lil 50 was running it. So far, things was running smoothly. Diva and Infamous was making plans to stack a few hundred thousand and go legit. Diva had been taking night classes to get a realtor's license. They say the future was in real estate. Diva had always been good with numbers and investing. They was in the process of looking for their own home to buy. They hadn't agreed on where just yet. Diva wanted to leave the Harris Country area and live on the outskirts of Houston. But Infamous was H-Town bred, and H-town fed anywhere outside the "H," he wouldn't be led! So everything was on hold.

…

"I think I'm pregnant!" Diva said cautiously, sitting down next to me our bed. She was holding a flat black smooth stomach. I looked from her belly, to her eyes and back to her belly. Then back to her eyes.

"What makes you think that? "I asked carefully. I wasn't

against her being pregnant, I just wanted to know what made her think what she thought.

"I missed my period," she responded. Dealing with females and their bodies is weird and confusing.

"Haven't that happened a few times before?" I asked trying not to upset her, but genuinely wondering, knowing this is more than the second time we done had the 'Baby, I'm pregnant,' discussion.

"Yea. But I been throwing up and shit," she said., "Then I been having dizzy spells. This right here is the real deal!" she offered. I looked at her. I didn't want to get excited for nothing. I really wanted a mini-me, a little soldier to carry my bloodline, to keep the Infamous legacy alive. To improve and make us royalty.

"Take one of them tests," I told her stating the obvious. That would be the smart thing to do. That or go see a doctor I thought.

"I don't need no test, I know my body!" I looked at her. "Really! If you knew your body so well, you wouldn't 'think' you were pregnant. You would know!!"

She sucked her teeth and stood up from the bed. I watched as she examined her body. As she picked up and dropped her titties, they did look fuller and heavier. I noticed her face was rounder, too.

"What you don't want no baby!" She asked looking over at me.

"Shut the fuck up! You sound real crazy!" I say, going back to the paperwork I was doing before she interrupted me.

"Well you act like you got a problem or something." Diva sounded like she was ready to argue. I had too much to do to entertain her foolishness so I ignored her as she stomped around the room. After throwing things around and making unnecessary noise for about 30 minutes she seen that I wouldn't take the bait so she chilled out and left the

134

bedroom. I could hear her in the front room on the phone. Unable to concentrate on my work, I decided to just get out the house and just go for a ride.

…

I winded up in 3rd ward. Had to see what the hood block niggas was on. Even though me and Diva was trying to get legit, we would always be street and hood. Niggas move to be new places but they never change faces. I knew I'd always be a street nigga!

"What it is, Infamous?!" Jody greeted me with a dap. This was the drank house! You could get it by the pint or you could get it by the later.

"Shit! just had to show face. See how you niggas was maintaining," I responded emphatically. Sade played from hidden speakers somewhere. A few familiar faces lounged around the small living room. I nodded at the people I knew and chucked the duce to the ones that I didn't.

"We still on money," my potna June Bug said coming from a backroom with a yellowbone stripper whose clothes and hair looked disheveled. We gave each other dap.

"Yu name been ringin' like always. But this time it's been ringing differently," He said looking me up and down. I had picked up a little weight.

"They say you got you a new lil momma who makes Lil Pus look like a little girl scout," I Smiled at that truth.

"Yeah,. I got a Diva!" I responded.

"Well the streets talking and they ain't talking bad!"

"You know I stay on my G shit."

Jody came and caught me an eight-ounce cup. I found me a spot to cop a squat and I took a sip of the oil. Candy sweet I smacked my tongue.

"I see you nigga's still mixin' and fixin' that good shit," I complimented Jody smiled and lifted his styrofoam cup up in a mock toast.

"In the trey we stay on the pay! He capped and laughed.

"What you got yo hands in now. The streets say that you done become a business man!" with that, everybody started looking and really paying attention to me.

"I'm just cruising my lane and staying out of everybody else's!" I responded. The game had been good to me. I was in the county tripping not long ago. Trippin' that I hadn't excelled in the game like I knew could. I had been getting money. Fucking hood rats and couldn't even pay for a decent lawyer when I had eventually landed in custody behind some real fluke shit. I felt like a real scrub and I made a vow that when I got out, I'd be 'bout my scratch. I would take my hustle to new heights and of course my plans had induced my potna Pat,but he had sold a nigga out like a 2 cent bag of Funyuns.

"What 's up with lit Pus?" I asked. I hadn't heard nothing about her in a while. Jody and June Bug both looked at me with weird expressions. June Bug was the first to speak.

"You didn't hear about her," He asked glancing at Jody.

"What happened ?" I reacted raising my voice.

"Man, some 5th ward nigga twisted her cap a couple of months ago," June Bug answered.

"They had been fucking around. When she caught the nigga creeping, she called the laws on that boy and told them he had drugs and a pistol on him," he explained.

"Well the nigga made bail got out and put two in her temple. Bet she won't do that again!" Damn. I hadn't heard about that. But I knew it was true because what he described was Lil Pus's 'M.O. she had done the Same thing to me a long time ago.

"What's the beef between you and yo' brother?" he asked referring to Pat I know that question was coming I was really tired of the subject.

136

"You gotta ask Pat." I responded June Bug and Jody exchanged glances. Exchanged glances.

"Whatever the beef is you nigga too good for that," Jody spoke. I stirred my drank and took a sip. I didn't want to get into no conversation about Pat. Even though I thought it was fucked up how he changed and switched up on me, I still didn't hate him. Neither did I want to talk down on him while he wasn't around!

"I'm just living my life. Trying to establish and Build me a legacy. yesterday is gone, Today is present and ready to be molded!" I said moving on.

"Y'all know any hoes that want to work at this butt naked I got?" I asked changing the subject. Might as well network while I was here.

"I need some fresh faces!" June Bug shook his head.

"I got two cousins that be selling' Pussy. I'm sure they'll went to get down." Judy said. "Give them my number and tell them to contact me. The sooner the better!"

When I got back to the apartment. Diva was asleep on the bed on top the sheets. She was stretched out naked. She had always been a wild hard sleeper. She had hair partially covering her face. She was snoring softly with her mouth opened. She looked so sexy even as she slept. I brushed the hair off her forchead and off her eyes. I let my eyes roam over her body. She was still thick and firm. I wandered then about the weight she would pickup once her pregnancy progressed   would the thickness turn to flab. Right now she was built like a stallion. I thought about waking her up with my tongue between her thighs and the pressure of my thumb and forefinger on her clit. She had awaken me so many times with my seed spilling down her throat. Now I'm gonna let her sleep. I had something to put together.

…

"Diva. We need to talk!!" Diva frowned at the look in Red's

eyes as she entered their apartment. Diva was in daisy dukes and a halter top. She had just finished doing her toenails. She had answered the door walking on the heel of her feet with cotton balls between her toes. She closed the door behind her and glanced down the hallway towards the bedroom where Infamous was on the phone with one of the workers from one of their butt naked houses.

"What's wrong girl!" Diva asked. Following Red to the couch where she sat down heavily. When Diva sat down next to Red, she noticed the Red puffiness of her eyes. This caused her to frown even deeper. Red was no crier so something was definitely wrong.

"Champagne just told me that she's been cheating on me. "Red voice broke. Diva wrapped Red in her arms. Red tensed up at first, her body going rigid. Then a second later she melted against Diva. Her face falling into a mask of tears. Diva just held her.

"Shhhh! Its alright." She whispered softly against the side of Red's face. That seemed to make Red cry harder.

"Whhhyyy!" she blubbered. "Oh. God I. I... I'm gon' gon' die!" she cried.

"Shhh! Shhh!" Diva repeated rocking Red in her arms trying to comfort her. Diva's mind was on Champagne. She had noticed change in Champagne. She was always acting strange. Something that Diva couldn't really pinpoint. It really wasn't no big issue people stray away and cheat. Its human nature to dip and creep.

"It ain't that bad Red." Diva said when Red calmed down. "I can't believe she would fuck over me like that!" Red sniffled whipping snot from her face with the back of her shirt sleeve.

"She don't want to tell me who it is. She say that its not another female though." Red eyes was swollen. This was Diva's first time seeing her cry like this. She knew now just

138

how deeply she felt fat champagne.

"It want be the same no more D!" Red whinnied. She looked into Diva's eyes. The pain quickly being replaced with anger.

"I won't be able to trust her no more. That's dead!"
Infamous came from the bedroom. He looked from Diva to Red. He saved her tear streaked face and Red eyes. He saw the look in Diva eyes and made a detour to the kitchen. He wanted no parts of 'Boo.hoo' session. He fixed himself a small snack in the kitchen and quickly turned back to the bedroom.

"I would never have done that to her "Red said sadly. Diva didn't know what to say. All she could do was listen and try to comfort her friend.

"I know, I…" Diva agreed looking at Red sympathetically. She felt helpless to help. But she was also curious as to who it was the dude that Champagne had cheated with. Both Red and Champagne had sworn off men. They had been fucked over time and time again. Abused verbally and physically, they were professed women scorned. Red sniffed and sighed deeply. Diva watched as she struggled to compose herself. She literally seen her get a grip.

"I'll forgive her, but I'll never be able to forget this shit." Red said straightening up. She pushed all of her hurt and sadness away. What's done was done
Gone away was yesterday! She turned and looked into Diva's eyes. She stared at her for a long moment.

"Thank you for being a friend and giving me your shoulder and ear." Red said thankfully. Diva just shrugged it off.

"Bitch, please! Don't even try that shit" Diva teased. Red broke into a wide smile. She hugged Diva strongly for a couple of long seconds.
She kissed her on the cheek.

"In another life you'd be my wife!! They both laughed hard.

Chapter 20

I was walking out the front door of the buttnaked house. I had opened a few months ago. It was in the nickel. It was making so much money I had to come see what made it so successful. Diva and Red had hired all the girls. I had no parts of that process. That's what had me investigating. I had chosen the location and that's it.' A lot of the girls that worked there were either ex-lovers, friends of associates of Champagne and Red. Coming out the front door I immediately got this funny feeling in my stomach. My belly became hollow and I got this sour acid taste in my throat. Outside cars was lined down the block It was like every house on the block had a function jumping.

"I wanna be a Diva doll!" This young girl looking no older than 15 stepped up in front of me. She had next to nothing on her small petite body. I frowned a little glassy eyed from the syrup and sweets.

"Who the fuck are you?" from the corner of my eye I saw movement. Before I could grasp what was exactly going on. I was surrounded by masked goons.

"nigga we want it all clothes jewelry and drawers!" One of the dudes said threateningly. Putting a big block clock between my eyes.

"What the fuck, are you serious!" Before I could say or do anything else the hard butt of the gun came down on my noses.

"Awww shittt!" I screamed grabbing my crooked nose, I knew my shit was broken. Muthafucker!

"nigga don't ask no questions just act!" I felt my 2 chains beings snatched from around my neck. I tried to look around and remember everything I could about my victimizers. Any mannerisms height, voice or body odor. Somebody was gonna pay for this shit.

"You thought you was gonna eat greedy forever and not get taxed by the gat, boys?" My nose was killing me. My vision kept becoming blurry. Whom! Another blow struck the side of my head.

"Shit!" I cursed and doubled over. I felt hands pushing me to the ground. Not wanting to fall to the ground and take the chance of being stamped out. My warrior spirit kicked in. I swung and struck the nearest body.

"Muthafucka!" I heard the masked man curse as my hard fist struck his fleshy jaw. I heard a gun cock and back twice Bywaz! Bywaz!. It first felt like I had been hit by two round stones. Then my skin immediately began to burn. It felt like somebody was sticking out in pain. I fell to the ground holding my side where I knew I had been shot. I heard people screaming and suddenly there was pure pandemonium. Gun fire erupted everywhere. Boom! Boom! Pow! Pow! Dat! Dat! Dat! People were running screaming. I was trying to curl myself into a knot and not get stampeded! My side and stomach was on fire. I felt my own Blood soaking my thin jersey. I had come to the house by myself. It couldn't be no random robbery because all they snatched was my chains. They didn't go through my pockets. They had other intentions. I guess they didn't expect me to fight back. That move threw their plans for a loop. I heard glass breaking and smelled smoke.

I knew these muthafuckas weren't burning me out.

"Infamous, Infamous?" I heard somebody screaming my name. I was in too much pain to respond. It felt like all the blood was leaking out of my body. I felt myself setting lightheaded. I knew I had lost a lot of Blood and was loosing blood still. Suddenly a familiar face was leaning over me looking me in my eyes.

"Pat"

"Infamous" I studied his eyes. What was he doing here. Where did he come from. He hadn't been there when I first arrived.

"Where are you shot at?" Pat asked looking over my blood-soaked clothes.

"Fuu.. Fuuu…" I tried to move my body so I could get up. Every small movement sent intense pain through my body.

"Just lay here the ambulance is on the way!" He said not touching me. He kept looking around nervously.

"Do you got our heat on you?" He asked looking down at me. I had left my pistol in my car.

"No, call Diva for me, hurry!" I said forcing myself to a sitting position. I started looking around me. All of sudden I didn't feel comfortable or safe being so close to Pat. That was weird my body started hyperventilating. I couldn't breath. I started chocking. I started seeing shit.

"Infamous, hold on baby!" I thought I seen Diva's face and felt her touch.

"It's okay baby. I told you I got you!" I kept blinking in and out of consciousness. While I was facing in and out. I kept seeing Diva, Champagne, Red. I saw a few unfamiliar faces. They were talking to me. Then I felt my clothes being ripped away. I felt myself wanting to fight the people that was trying to steal my clothes. I was too weak. Then oil of a sudden I was out.

I came to the sounds of the hospital machines beeping as soon as I came to the pain hit me. It felt like the inside of my stomach was on fire. The first face I seen was Diva's. Her tear streaked face had dried blood on it. Concerned that she had been hurt also somehow. I tried to speak. My mouth was drier than the Sahara Desert. The only thing that came out of my mouth was a croaking sound.

"Shhh!" Diva jumped up and covered my lips with one of her fingers.

"Don't try to talk. Just get well. We got business to handle." She sounded so tough. But her eyes showed fear and pain. Again, I tried to talk but no words came out of my mouth only a dry animal sound. Too weak. The little effort I used to try communicate with Diva drained me and sent me back to lala land.

When I awakened again the doctor was standing over me with one of those eye lights trying to sear my pupils it seemed.

"Ah! You're awake!" I frowned no shit!

"How're you feeling Mr. Johnson?" He asked. He was pale faced with blue eyes that look like those marbles. I use to play with as a kid. He was looking at me intently. I produced enough saliva to dampen my parched throat and let him know I needed to be hydrated. I looked around for Diva. But she wasn't there which gave me a bad feeling. The doctor grabbed a small pitcher of iced water from the rolling stand that sat next to the hospital bed I was laying in. He retrieved a new straw and placed it in the pitcher and held it to my mouth so. I could drink.

"Drink slow!" He coached pulling the pitcher away when I took a greedy pull on the straw and almost chocked. I felt like I was swallowing wet needles.

There you go!" He said smoothly as I got my fill and laid my head back on the soft pillow. I sighed. I saw movement

144

out the side of my eyes and then heard a squeal.

"Oh my God Baby!" Diva almost threw herself on me but stopped short. I smiled weakly at her.

"Nigga you ever scare me like this again…." She let her words trail off. She touched my forehead. The doctor cleared his throat.

"Excuse me." He chuckled. "Let me finish my examination. Then I'll give y'all a movement Mr. Johnson. But only a minute because he needs to rest. He lost quite a lot of Blood. "The doctor said. He came forward putting the stethoscope to my chest checking my heartbeat and my chest. I had been shot twice in the stomach a close blank range. I was lucky they had missed any vital organs. The doctor said if the bullets would've landed a few centimeters down I would have been sporting one of those fancy shit bags. Thank God for small favors.' He felt me up a little but more. I felt a heavy sensation on my groin area. When I looked down, I saw the tube from the catheter running from my dick shit!

"What the fuck is that doc..?" I said pointing at the tube running between my legs.

"It's only temporary. Once you get your strength, we can remove it." He reassured me pointing my leg carefully.

I frowned down at the tube coming from my manhood.

"Do my shit still work?" I asked feeling funny. I glanced over at Diva. She was listening raptly. The doctor smiled.

"The tube is only inserted because you weren't conscious. To keep you from urinating on yourself we gave you the catheter." He explained.

"You still didn't answer my question!" I responded. I was watching him closely.

"Do my shit still work?" I couldn't do nothing with that erectile dysfunction shit. I was too young to have a broke dick. The doctor chuckled.

"You should be good. But we won't be for sure for a couple

of days yet."

"A couple of days. I'm not staying in this bitch another day." I argued.

"We need to run some more test. We need to monitor your healing progress. Make sure you don't develop any immediate infections." I wasn't feeling this shit.

"How long is that supposed to take?"

"A week or so!"

"A week!!!" The doctor frowned at me and I looked at Diva.

"Just chill out!" she said walking up to the bed and putting her warm soft hand on mine.

"These people know what they doing," she reassured me. The doctor answered a few more questions poked and probed at a couple of spots on my body. Then he lift me and Diva by ourselves.

"A detective has been up here like three times." Diva began. Her eyes were glassy and tired.

"They keep askin' foolish questions like we ain't gone keep this shit in the street!" I looked at her.

"Y'all know who did this shit!" I asked feeling so many emotions attack me at once.

"We got a good idea, but you won't like it nor agree with it" Diva said already doubting my confidence in her.

"Who did it" Diva looked at me a long moment and then said.

"The word is Pat ordered some random hood Flunkies to take you down a notch!" 'Take me down a notch!' I looked at Diva. What the hell was that supposed to mean? She was right I didn't like or agree with what she said. I know me and Pat wasn't talking because he was tripping on some "my girl" shit but we wasn't beefin'. That nigga didn't hate me enough to harm me like this. He wouldn't orchestrate something as vicious as this.

"Now momma, you right! I don't agree!" I responded

146

killing that assumption before it got along to far.

"Don't be gullible and stupid Infamous!" Diva warned, she didn't understand Pat was my brother from another mother we had grew up together. We had been closer than air and earth. We had gone our separate ways. Did our thing. He didn't like that me and Diva was 1 but he wouldn't never go out like this. I could and wouldn't believe that Pat would do this to me. Then I had a flash back to this moment I had come to. Pat was there standing above me was that an illusion? I thought I had seen Diva too. He had been right there. He could've did me in quickly.

"Was you at the house?" I asked Diva.

"I had showed up later because he had called me and said you was shot!"

Chapter 21

"Where you been?" Red asked. She was looking at Champagne suspiciously. Champagne frowned throwing her car keys on the nightstand and sitting down on the bed where Red was sitting cross legged, rolling a blunt.

"I was out doin' what I do!" Champagne responded. She tossed a roll of bills onto the covers and began pulling her shoes off.

"God" Champagne sighed laying back on the bed. Red looked down at her. She studied her face and closed eyes.

"Why you so tired!" Red asked. Champagne forehead wrinkled up. Her eyes slowly came open and found Red's.

"Don't start that shit Red!" Champagne complained. She looked at Red angrily. Red held eye contact.

"I'm not starting nothing!" Champagne blew air out of her mouth and rose up from the position she had laid. She looked back at Red. She knew Red had a reason. But still. Yeah. She had fucked up and got twisted up with Pat. But she had confessed that transgression and dropped that. She had been faithful ever since. Why was Red still tripping.

"I had made a couple of moves trying to get some chedda for you. So why you on that trip shit." Champagne argued.

"I don't know what you been doing. You ain't called or sent

149

me a text or nothing." Red complained. She finished rolling the blunt and stood up from the bed.

"Let's not do this!"

"Now let's do this" Red was feeling bitchy.

"Get it our yo system!" Champagne said throwing up her hands.

"Go' head get it out. Whatever you gotta do!!"

"What you talkin' about?" Red asked. She was watching Champagne from the other side of the bed.

"Whatever it is you goin' through!" Champagne responded. "I'm tired of this shit. I fucked up once and you act like I went out and fucked a whole nation of niggas and bitches!" Champagne looked at Red with frustration in her eyes.

"I admitted my fuck up. You didn't find out about it from the streets. I told you!"

"That don't mean shit!" Red yelled.

"Then you don't even want to tell me who it was. That's same bullshit! So you still got a secret!" Champagne looked away. How could she get Red past her fuck up? Will she ever forget that shit?

"You might got you a sugar daddy somewhere. I don't know. If you lie once you'll lie twice!" Red said angrily.

"That's what you still trippin' on. Cause you don't know who it was!" Champagne sighed.

"That's so petty!" Red was in the act of putting the blunt to her mouth. She paused dramatically.

"Petty! Petty! Bitch, you cheated on me. You went out and played with some dick. While I been reppin'," Red yelled. "Bitch you betrayed me not once, not twice. But several times!" Red had forgotten all about the blunt that was burning in her hand. Wearing only panties, no bra. Her hair wild in a big curly fro bouncing with her angry movements. "Y'all just wasn't fuckin', you didn't just dip off and get some dick or some pussy. You and whatever nigga it was

150

had a thing, like some secret lover shit goin' on. Red put the blunt out. "And I still don't know who the nigga is!!" Champagne threw her hands in the air then slapped her thighs.

"What's so important that you have to know who the nigga is that fucked me???" Champagne responded, Red caught her eyes. Champagne just didn't get it! Red picked the blunt back up and was preparing to relight it when Champagne dropped the bomb.

"Okay, I was lettin' Pat dig my back out!" Champagne screamed. It's like the whole world stopped. Red paused with the blunt at her lips. She started screaming like a wild banshee. She hopped over the bed and started attacking Champagne.

"R.R..R..Reedd!!" Champagne stuttered. She was trying to block the blows that Red was fiercely throwing. Red was screaming and punching. Champagne was trying to protect her face. The first blow had her struck her eye and she felt her eye swell on contact. Now she was trying to protect her face, Red was wild. She was hurting and she was out of control.

"Bitch! How Dare You!" Red said raining blows down on Champagne who had fell against the bed. Red tried to burn Champagne with the blunt she had in her hand.

"I'll kill you bitch!!" Red stopped she climbed off of Champagne.

"Red, no!" Champagne screamed jumping up and tackling Red on the bed. They began wrestling Champagne knew that Red was attempting to go get the gun that they kept in the bedroom's closet.

"Let me up bitch!" Red argued struggling to get away from Champagne.

"Calm the fuck down!" Champagne yelled holding tightly to Red. She knew if Red reached the closet and got the gun she would try to kill her.

"Bitch I am gone kill you. Get …off…me !!" Red struggled under Champagne. All of a sudden she just quit resisting. Champagne still holding on to her looked down. She heard Red sniff. Then watched as her body became racked with sobs.

"I'm so sorry baby!" Champagne said her own eyes filling up with water she pulled Red into her arms and held her tightly.

"I'm so sorry!" Champagne repeated holding and sucking Red in her arms. All Red could do was cry. She squeezed Champagne shirt and soaked her with her hurt and betrayal.

"Why, why?" Red sniffed.

"Shhhhh!" Champagne shushed her and rocked her in her arms. After a few minutes, Red's tears began to subside. Champagne kept rocking her like a little baby. Red pulled out of Champagne 's arms.

"Why 'Pagne?" Red asked. Her eyes red and swollen with pain. Champagne stared back speechless. One of her eyes puffy and black from the first blow Red had delivered. She had a busted lip and scratches across her face. Champagne just shook her head of the question. She didn't have an answer. She didn't know she had got, caught up in the moment with Pat. It all started from the first night they had all hooked up. She had felt the same energy for Pat that Diva had left for Infamous. Something about both of their vibes she had gotten caught up. At first she had just wanted to feel him. The heat of his sexual organ. She had just wanted to be fucked by him. But after their session and he had fucked her so good. She couldn't help but go back after seconds and thirds and fourths. The beef between Pat and Infamous was of little or no cord to her. She just wanted Pat's dick.

152

"I am sorry Red" Champagne whispered looking Red in the eyes. Her sincerity dipped from her whole being.

"I didn't mean to hurt you, Red!!" They stared at each other and few long moments. All of a sudden Red's face twisted with a tan of anger and hate. She hacked up a big glop of spit and spit into Champagnes eyes.

"Get out Bitch! Get the fuck out my house!" Red roared. Champagne head flew back. A look of total disbelief came over her face. Red jumped up from the bed again and headed in the direction of the closet. This time Champagne didn't do no hesitating. She jumped up and ran in the opposite direction. Buzz! Buzz! Buzz! Red shot 3 times. Champagne screamed and barely made it out the door. When the bullet struck and splintered the wood.

"Oh shit!" Champagne screamed. She rushed out of the apartment. She heard Red hollering and threatening.

"I'm gone kill you bitch!"

…

"Deeper daddy!" Diva moaned. Her black skin was sweating and damn near turning me on even more than the tight wet sensation of her pussy.

"Damn girl," I breathed moving slowly in and out of her. Diva to me always had the body of a Ghetto goddess. I stroked her body. Our eyes were locked on each other. Our connection so great and feeling so perfect. I pushed into her. Her calves were on my shoulder and I had a pillow propped into her.

"Fuck.. me… daddyyy… Oh shit.. come… on," Diva started pushing her pelvis up to meet my thrusts.

"This what you want momma!!" I responded picking up my pace.

"Oooohh Shiii…" Just when I was about to rise to my peak we were threw off by a pounding on the front door.

"What the fuck??" We both yelled simultaneously jumping

apart automatically. I reached for my pistol that was on the nightstand. Diva started reaching for her clothes.

"Who the fuck?" I said angrily. Pulling on boxers. A large tent making my movements awkward. I looked at Diva who had threw on a T-shirt and shorts. I began walking to the front door to see who the fuck was pounding on my door and looked out and saw Red standing there with a disheveled looked. A little of my anger died down. But only for a second.

"What's wrong, Red" I asked concern in my voice.

"I just had a fight with Champagne!!" I looked at Red for a long moment was this bitch serious?? I looked back at Diva who was coming out of the bedroom.

"You what?" I had to make this bitch repeat herself. I know I just didn't hear her say what I thought she said. She just didn't come interrupt my groove with no bullshit!

"I had a fight with Champagne and I shot at her!!" Red repeated. I looked at Diva. Her eyes begging me not to bug out. Before I could, Diva came and wrapped Red in her arms. They hugged each other for a long moment. Red was looking over Diva's shoulder. I guess she smelled the sex on Diva. She glanced down and saw the semi –hardness that still tented my boxers.

"I'm sorry y'all" Red apologized figuring now that she had interrupted us. I just walked to the bathroom to take a cold shower. I know this was gonna turn out to be a long night. I got the feeling that what we had started was over with. When I came out of the shower. Diva and Red was in the living room with the Radio blasting and the room clouded with blunt smoke. I was ready to ride out my vibe was broken and over with. I had put on some clothes grabbed my truck keys and was ready to go check on one of the new buttnaked house I had opened up in homestead.

"Where you going? Diva asked when I made it to the living

room.

"I gotta go check on that new house "Diva looked at me for a minute. I guess she was trying to figure if I was upset.

"Sit down Infamous!" Diva said and I frowned, seeing my frown she just Patted the seat beside her on the couch. Red was laid out on the floor. her hair in a wild curly afro.

"I'm sorry bro!" she apologized. "What up?" I asked sitting down.

'Champagne told Red that she had been cheating on her with Pat!" I looked down at Red who was looking at me with fire in her eyes.

"Oh yeah!" I responded not knowing what else to say All of sudden Pat had become enemy I. My mind still could not wrap around the fact he had something to do with me getting shot. I knew me and the then nigga wasn't tight no more because he wanted. Diva and she wanted me. But to want to see me physically harmed.

"Red and her fought and Red shot at her," Diva said I looked at Red with raised eyebrows.

"Fuck the bitch!" she spit with venom, "Not only did she sleep with the enemy she violated several unwritten codes!" I seen the fire in Red's eyes and was glad she was on our team.

"I'm gone kill that bitch!" I looked over at Diva who just looked at me and shrugged.

"Is she seein' Pat?" I asked. Red face balded up into a mask of fury.

"It don't matter. One time is too many!" Red shot.

"She shot at Champagne." Diva cut in. "So you know Champagne is gonna go back and tell Pat. Even if they're not together!" Diva needed her head.

"I mean who else do she got now?!"

"That don't mean Pat gonna fuck with her again" I said.

"I mean didn't they part ways when she got an attack of the

guilty conscious." Diva looked at Red who had risen from her lazy slouched position on the floor.

"Hell fuck with her because Champagne is a grimy bitch!!" Red said.

"They may come together and try to bring you down!" I frowned.

"Me!!!" I looked over at Diva then back at Red.

"What beef do I have with Champagne!" I asked. Diva frowned too.

"Yeah what does Infamous got to do with you and Champagne's shit?" Diva asked.

"We been hustlin' together. Pat can pick Champagne's brain and learn how you been moving and what you going!! Everybody got quiet. I was thinking about what Red said. Did it make sense. It really did.' How the fuck did sugar turn this shitty? All I knew I'd forever be on my top of game. Shit was getting crucial. I had been shot. I wasn't trying to go through the shit no more. I knew I had a lot of enemies out there now. One was the nigga that knew how I thought.

"Fuck that shit. Nan one of them mufuckas won't catch me slippin.' I said looking from Diva to Red back to Diva.

"Are you alright Red?" I asked. She looked alright on the outside. But I know inside she had to be fucked up. Love was a muthafucka. We talked hard but when your heart was bleeding inside shit wasn't sweet.

"I'm good!" Red said.

"If you need a place to rest you know you always welcomed here!" I said studying her eyes.

"Than you?"

"You family momma!" I got up from the couch and was headed out of the house.

"How long you gone be gone?" Diva asked getting up and coming to the door where I had paused.

156

"Probably a couple of hours!" I responded. Diva put her arms around my neck. We kissed softly as she looked in my eyes.

"You need to hurry back we got unfinished business." She bit me on the bottom lip.

Chapter 22

Pat looked deeply into Champagne eyes. He was trying to figure out if he could trust her or not. She had shown up on his doorstep. She was shaking with tears pouring down her face. He could barely understand her. She was blubbering, slanging snot and not making sense. When he had finally gotten her to calm down. She had explained the fight she had with Red she told him that Red had shit at her. That's what made him start paying attention. But all this shit could be a set up. It could be a hoax in retaliation to what had happened to Infamous a few months ago. Word was already out that ever go one thought that Pat if not the shooter knew who had took the shots that put Infamous in the hospital. Maybe they were trying to set at him. Right now they were pillow talking. She had been with him for the last two days. "I ain't got nobody!" Champagne said softly. Pat at first just stared at her.

"How can I trust ya?" Pat asked bluntly and honestly. This shit was real. It wasn't no book or movie. He was looking at Champagne seriously and deeply. Champagne just looked at him not saying nothing at first.

"I know we didn't begin on no square honest type shit. But I'm not all that rotten!" Champagne began.

"I'm not here to try an set you up for Infamous or nobody on that side." She was looking Pat directly in his eyes as she spoke.

"That chapter of my life is done." She said sincerely.

"I was in love with Red but she did the ultimate no no she tried to shoot me." Champagne looked off at a spot on the wall remembering the sounds of that gun going off. Hearing the hard thumps as the bullets struck the door by her head as she ran off. She still had a deep gash disfiguring the side of her face. A sharp piece of world had cut her deeply.

"I had told her. Being honest with her. That I had fucked you and this is what I get for my honesty. Fuck Red and everybody she ride for!" Champagne spit. Pat listened and felt Champagne's body shake with anger. He smiled inside. But outside his face remained impassive.

"So what you gone do?" Pat asked looking down at Champagne. Champagne frowned.

"What do you mean?" she asked slightly confused.

"Wasn't you livin with Red?" Pat asked. Champagne looked up into Pat's eyes understanding his question.

"I'm ready to ride with you!" she said they looked at each other for a long moment.

"I'm the original Down ass bitch!" Pat kept studying her eyes.

"Whatever you want. Whatever you say. Whatever the game. I'm gone play." Champagne said snuggling up against Pat.

"You know your gone have to prove yourself first right!?" Pat said bluntly. Champagne looked up at him and just nodded her head.

...

Diva was closing up the shop. It was dusk. The sky was pinkish and purple as the sun was setting. It was Monday and she was closing at the appointed early time. Every

Monday they closed at 6:30 p.m. Everybody had already left. She had locked the says money and requests into the hidden safe in the back office. Her Louis Vuitton purse was heavy from the pistol that she kept. She saw a shadow through the glass. Before she could turn, she was hit in the back of the head hard. Immediately she fell to the floor dizzy.

"Bitch you think you invisible!" A voice said harshly over her. Diva was dizzy and disoriented. She tried to shake her head and felt blood drip down the back of her neck. She reacted to the feel and was hit again in the mouth. She felt her two front teeth immediately broke.

"Awwww." She screamed reaching up, covering her mouth. The masked gunman jacked her purse away, grabbed a handful of her hair.

"Y'all think y'all got a solid team?" He growled.

"Give a message to Infamous for me." He threw her head away from him. He gave her 3 vicious kicks.

"Prepare to be eradicated and destroyed piece by piece!" He said kicking and spitting on Diva. She just curled into a fetal position and tried to protect herself as much as possible praying for oblivion.

…

Hell now! These niggas was playing with death now. They done fucked with my baby. I was speeding down Almeda. I was pushing the ford to the max all 240 horses was galloping. I had tears in my eyes and murder in my heart! I had gotten a call on my phone from one of the white women that worked next to the shop. She had been hysterical. She had said Diva had been pistol whipped and assaulted. She had been coming to the door of her clothing boutique to switch a window display out when she witnessed. A tell stocky person of unknown nationality wearing a mask and dark clothing. He had been kicking and punching on Diva.

When she saw him she began pounding on the glass of her store. He had paused and pointed a gun and shot at the glass. She had ducked back in and went and called "H.P.D" She didn't wait. She grossed a baseball but that she kept in her back office. But when she had got back to the front he was gone. When she went out to Diva she was still breathing but unconscious. Her whole face was swollen and bloody. Her clothes were ripped. But she was breathing. The lady had stayed with Diva until the police and paramedics arrived. Diva refused to go to the hospital or cooperate with the police. So her neighbor had reached me on my cell phone. I almost didn't answer the unknown number. Now I was headset to the "Woodlands." The place where the white woman lived and had taken Diva too!!. Muthafuckas done crossed a line It's war. I had been focused on getting money now the gun has been brought to life. Not somebody was gonna pay. But a lot of somebodies was gonna pay. They went too farr!! They didn't fuck with my money. They fucked with my heart. I tried to prepare myself for what I was about to see with Diva. I prayed that she wasn't messed up too bad. That her face didn't have no permanent disfigurements.

When I pulled up to the two-story house. I had no time to look and enjoy the grandiosity of the place. I jumped out of my truck and ran to the front door. Before I could even knock or ring the doorbell. The door fled open. A little pigtailed girl was looking up at me with big wide green eyes.

"Hello, is my wife Diva here!?" I asked looking around her into the big house. I couldn't see nothing past a deep foyer and a long hallway. A winding staircase.

"What are you?" she asked. I really didn't have no time for no snotty nosed rung cats.

"Is my wife h…" Before I could repeat my question. A Tom

162

Cruise look alike appeared out of nowhere.

"Excuse me." He said pushing the little girl to the side and reaching a hand out of me.

"Ashley find something o occupy you." He dismissed the little girl.

"Sir. I'm Torey. Follow me!" He said shaking the hand I extended and then turn and led me to the left to what looked like a den. Diva was laying down on a love seat. The thin white woman had several wet bloody towels covering her head and face. My heart started beating wildly as I approached her side. The white woman looked up and saw my face and slowly stood to her feet. She approached me with tears running down her face. She embraced me, hugging me tightly.

"I gave her a mild sedative she's dozing now. She said searching my eyes.

"It's bad. She didn't want them to take her to the hospital. But I think she may have a concussion." I said nothing. I looked at the bloody towels over Diva's head. It looked like they had tried to clean her up the best they could. But her lips were looking like twin ballons. They were caked with blood. My heart welled with rage. A rage I had never known. I felt these strange white people eyes on me. But I refused to look at them. My eyes stayed glued to Diva. Her eyes were black and blue and closed. Boiling with rage my hands shook as I touched Diva's hand that was folded onto her chest. Feeling my touch only one eye was not swollen shut. She looked at me with her one good eye that was clotted with blood on the inside. I watched her lips work trying to speak.

"Shhh! Momma. I'm here now!" I said reassuring her as I tenderly held her hand. I saw a lone tear slide out the side of her eye.

"I know D. shhhhh! I got you ma on my life!!!" I got tired of choking back the tears and trying to be brave in front of these white follies. I allowed my eyes to spring a leak. I felt her squeeze my hand weakly trying to comfort me which made the situation worse. Before I know it. I was on my knees with my head in Diva's lap. I felt her fingertips stroking my scalp. I took a deep breath and stood up. Torey and his wife were standing back at a distance. He was behind her rubbing her shoulders. I looked at his wife.

"First I want to thank you for being there for Diva" I aid sincerely.

"Also thank you for bringing her here to your home and carin' for her." I looked back at Diva who had drifted back off.

"No thanks needed" she responded.

"Is there anything you can tell me about the guy that did this?" I asked sounding like a detective from the movies. She began to shake her head then she paused.

"I can't describe him. But I did see him get into a dark blue Camry." She said. I stored that information in the back of my mind.

Chapter 23

I pulled up to Elgin and Westheimer. I parked my car and got out. It was time to walk. The first person I saw was my home girl Rachael.

"You didn't forget where the block was, did you?" she asked.

"Real niggas never forget where they come from." I responded.

"We may elevate in our game but we still acknowledge the rep from which we came!!"

"You always got something slick to say."

"I'm just statin' facts!" I walked up on the porch of the house in which she was sitting. I invited myself a seat. I had a agenda.

"You don't even come around no more. Like you done got too grand for the common folk!" Rachael said.

"I don't even know what 'grand' is other than the amount. Secondly when you reaching for the stars you can't get stretch to the ground." I looked Rachael in her eyes.

"I'll always be a hood nigga. My loyalty is written in blood!" Rachael continued to look at me. I seen that she was oblivious to the drama that was playing out in my life. Either she wasn't aware and a part of the conspiracy to disrupt my progress and shut me down or she was a pretty good actress.

"Tell me something Rachael!" I said looking at her.

"Have Pat been around on me?" Rachael shook her head. "That nigga don't even fuck with the lock no more!" She responded I let that sink in and got up preparing to leave.

"Well if you happen to see that nigga let him know all bets are off!" Rachael looked at me frowning.

"Whats goin' on?" she asked. If she didn't know by now she didn't need to know.

"Some grown and ganxta shit!"

...

I was heavy on the waist and I had a chip on my shoulder I roamed the block looking for answers and victims. I had a hard on to catch Pat or whoever he had shoot me and do what the did at my Buttnaked club. I wanted to catch and torture the individual that harmed Diva. Even though she was a product of the streets. She was still female. They didn't have to injure her like they did. I was gonna make sure whoever had did it was gonna suffer for what they did to her had promised that. I wasn't gonna rest until I find the culprits an destroy them mentally and physically. I never thought I would ever hate someone as much as I hated Pat and the people or person responsible for Diva's injuries.

"Infamous, what's up Big Money." P.A. was coming from Hyde Park when I ran into him. He had a large smile on his face. But I let my features remain neutral.

"It ain't easy when yo homies turn phony you don't know who to trust." I responded. P.A. frowned at the tune in my voice and the look in my eyes.

"What's good playa?" He asked searching my eyes.

"Somebody got at Diva and did her real dirty!" I explained. "They showed her no love an no mercy dog." P.A. frowned deeper and a look of disbelief entered his eyes.

166

"We ain't been on no grimy shit or nothing Just livin day by day." P.A. shook his head and asked.

"What happened?"

"They pistol whipped her. Knocked out her two front teeth and stomped her." My rage came boiling up just remembering the injuries to Diva's face and body.

"Damn cuzz seriously?" P.A. shook his head and studied me. I gave him a look.

"nigga's gone get it a thousand times worse." I said meaning every word I said.

"Do you know who did it?" He asked dumbly.

"I know Pat had something to do with it!" I answered P.A. frowned.

"You serious?"

"If you ask me if I'm serious one me time!"

"That nigga done flipped out like that!"

"He sold his soul for cheap now this shit done got deep not even the messiah himself can save that nigga nor the people he get close to!!!: P.A. looked at me a long time. I guess he saw the fires of hell burning in my eyes because he looked off.

"He ain't been around here in a minute." P.A. said after a while.

"When you see that nigga. Tell him to make sure he make it right with his creator. Kiss everybody he love, and make sure got his estate in order." Again P.A. looked at me a long moment. I guess he felt the heat of death coming off of me. Because he nodded his head and then took off at a fast pace. I know P.A. wasn't no scary nigga and my message would be delivered. My purpose now was to flush the niggas out that he paid to be triggermen. I know it was at least three different guys that came to the house for me. Then you had the one lone man that did the damage to Diva. That was 4 individuals not including Pat. I had enough anger, hate and

167

rage inside of me to execute a Taliban of niggas all by my lonely.

"Hello!"

'You know the nigga out touchin' the pavement askin questions!"

"Let him ask" There was a few seconds of silence.

"What you gone do?"

"What I been doin'. Grindin and pushin!!" Pat disconnected the call and sat his phone on the couch beside him. He had been smoking a blunt and watching music video's when that call came. Now he was looking at the red and not seeing the images on the screen. His mind now on the future. He knew Infamous. He knew now he had to face him. How they had reached this point he didn't know. But fuck Infamous. He wasn't afraid of the nigga. He had grew up with the nigga. He knew the way the nigga thought and how he moved. He probably knew the nigga better than he knew himself. Infamous was no big threat. The nigga was too soft. Pat sparked the blunt up and took a big pull. He contemplated his next move. He knew he had to be mentally 2 steps ahead of Infamous. It was now war Infamous fought with his mind first so he knew that's where the war began. Pat smiled to himself "Infamous the quiet one! The killer moving in silence!" Well you've been exposed killer!" Pat thought to himself. He felt the explosive high of the kush sweet hit him. He felt he was in a realm all it's own. "You ready nigga?" Pat said aloud in the silence of his bedroom. He took another strong take and hit himself in the chest hard like a gorilla. "Here I am, come get me!!!!"

...

"Who in the fuck is Infamous!!!" Keith roared. He was sitting in the back of the abandoned car. It was the regular spot that Keith sold pills out of everyday. The long stolen car with nothing left but the body and tore seats was parked

168

in the back of the "Sundance apartment complex handing outside the car was the usual suspects "Bam Bam, savage, and Face. Along with a few junkies that were trying to beg or work their way up on a fix.

"That nigga done put no fear in nobody heart!" Bam Bam and savage was just lounging and listening. While face spoke to Keith.

"I know that I was just saying."

"You was just saying what?? You sounded pussy tome!" Keith shot.

"I know what Infamous is apostle of and I was just tellin' you what the word was!" Face defended.

"The word is. The nigga lookin' for the niggas that shot up him and his house. Along with whoever beat the brakes off of his bitch." Keith cut in.

"That could be anybody in the whole world nigga" Keith featured. Nigga acted so stupid sometimes. People were their own biggest enemy. They didn't need nobody to put the finger on them. They often times told it on themselves.

"You said that to say what? A nigga should start shaking in his boots and lookin' over his shoulders like the phantom is after him!" Keith continued. Bam Bam and savage laughed. They weren't afraid of Infamous or even worried about him finding out that they had participated in the hit on him. Although their guns never turned in his direction, they still popped off the house.

"Face, you act like he the boogeyman or something!" Savage said laughing.

"You nigga's can make a joke out that shit of you want too!" Face shot back. Savage and Bam Bam exchanged a look. Before either one of them could say anything, Keith had jumped out of the car and placed his gun in the middle of Face's eyes.

"nigga you sound weak!" Keith said looking Face in his

eyes.

"You know what they say about weak links??" Face stared back at Keith with pleading eyes.

"nigga you the wink link?" Keith asked pushing the gun harder against his face. Face was afraid to move an inch. Afraid to open his mouth. He started to shake.

"Fuck Infamous nigga. You need to be afraid of me and what I'll do to you!" Keith mushed him with the gun and face stumbled backwards and fell on his ass. Savage and Bam Bam laughed at him.

"Get you weak ass out of here white I'm still letting you walk!" Keith spit. Face jumped up and hurried away. He looked over his shoulder a couple of times before he disappeared.

"You should've let that nigga have it. You might have fucked up!" Savage said watching Face disappear.

Him and Keith shared a look. Then Keith glanced over at Bam Bam.

"Yeah, you might've made a wrong decision!"

Chapter 24

"I told you. You should've shot em!" Diva said chuckling. "That's not funny D" I said. We were in our bedroom. Listening to Keith Sweat and just relaxing. I had smoked a sweet earlier and popped a 'k'. Diva was healing slowly but nicely. She still was missing her two front teeth which had her now talking with a slight lisp. She had a broken nose which Infamous had painfully reset. 2 or 3 cuts was scabbing over on her face, you could still see the blood clots inside her eyes. They had found out a couple of days ago that she was pregnant.

"Well I did!!" Diva continued and smiled at me. She threw one hand up to cover her mouth. Shy about the current state of her dental work. She looked real off but I wasn't gonna tell her that she had dealt with a serious situation. She still woke up at night screaming and shaking.

"I didn't know the nigga was capable of such rottenness." I said looking at Diva and chewing on a Newport. Another habit I had picked up us both smoking cancer sticks. I looked at Diva and shook my head.

"Didn't know the nigga so much envy and hatred in his heart. I mean what did we do to that nigga!"

Diva shrugged her shoulders. We were both at a loss. When

I had cut into Diva. Pat had been my right hand man. The Robin to my Batman. Now that nigga was wishing death upon me.

"You really don't know nobody like you think you do" Diva said looking off into space.

"Situations and circumstances change the heart of many men. The people you really thought were yo friends…" Her voice trailed off. I reached over across the bed and touched her shoulder. She looked back at me.

"I'm the real deal. The genuine article. I'll always be yo stand up nigga!" I said looking her in the eyes. I got up and walked around to her side of the bed and pulled her up into my arms. I kissed her lips gently. Looking into her eyes I gently laid her down on the bed.

"You just relax momma. Tell me at any moment if anything began to hurt." Diva sighed and closed her eyes. I started at her feet. I massaged and sucked her toes, licked the soles of her beautiful feet. Lifting one leg slightly in the air I nibble and bit at the back of her ankles. I listened to her body and the sounds she made. I nibbled, bit and suckled up her calves to the back of her knees and tights.

"How do you feel baby?" I asked only getting a mumble in response. I moved to her inner thighs. I knew how to make her talk to me. I inhaled the arousal between her legs. She was shaved, wet and ready to be devoured. First, I licked and sucked at the fleshy folds between her thighs.

"Ooohhh" she cooed spreading her legs farther apart. I wasn't ready to please her fully yet. I moved and dipped my tongue into her belly. Holding her waist gently I nibbled and bit at her sides. I nipped at the soft skin when I got to her firm breast. I twisted and pinched at her nipples.

"Yes daddy, please." She breathed, covering her titties with my mouth. I sucked at her nipples like a starved newborn.

"Ahhh baby, just like that!" she reached her back and pulled

172

my head deeper into her bosom so that the other breast wouldn't feel left out. I switched sides and gave it the equal amount of attention. The way that Diva was moaning and squirming my way between her thighs. My hard 9½ inches like a heat seeking missile stood at attention at her warm wet entranced.

"You ready baby?" I whispered pushing the head of my hard member between her pussy lips.

"Yes daddy cmon. I need you!" Diva breathed and pushed her pelvic up to meet me.

"Ahhh shit!" I cursed. She was so tight I pushed only a little ways into and worked my hips.

"Uuuuh Uuuhhhh!!" holding myself up with my arms I worked all 9½ inches into her tightness. She became soak and wet. Pulling her knees up to her titties I worked her into a frenzy.

"Au…au..ou..ohh… shi…shii…." I watched Diva's eye roll to the back of her head. She began to shake uncontrollably.

"I…. I'm… cu…hmm" I covered her lips with my own and sucked on her tongue and fucked her until I exploded. Diva flopping like a fish went from grabbing the sheets. To grabbing her hair to scratching my body. My body covered hers. Both of us wet with sweat was breathing like we had been running from the police for the last week.

"Get off me!" she breathed. I dragged my body to the side of the bed. Before I knew it, I was out like a light.

…

We had token a shower and was watching the news. It was 11 o'clock p.m. and we were laying in complete silence. There was a sudden knock at the front door. I grabbed the chrome 9 that I kept on the nightstand. I clicked the safety off as I walked to the front door. I was always on high alert. I looked out the door and saw Face. An old homey from the hood. I frowned and looked back at the bedroom. Diva was out of sight. Probably hadn't moved from her place on the bed. I opened the door with the gun pointed directly at him. My finger on the trigger. Itchy to pop something or somebody.

"What's up?" I asked simply Face threw his hands up in surrender.

"Whoa whoa!" he started. I pulled the nigga in the apartment and slung him on the floor quickly kicking the door closed behind me. I hit him in the head with the gun. Fuck it! Every nigga was a suspect and guilty until proven innocent.

"What you doin' at my door nigga? And how the fuck do you know where I stay nigga??" I asked ready to blow this nigga brains all over the carpet in my living room. I saw the fear of God in his eyes.

"Pppplease" He stuttered trying to sink into the floor.

"I..I..I just cccame to tell you… uhhh!" I had become impatient and hit him again with the gun.

"Nigga spit it out! What the fuck you doing at my house!" Diva had heard the commotion and came to the door of the front room. When she seen me holding the dude at gunpoint she had quickly closed the door.

"Keith and Bam Bam are the ones that shot you!" He said. I hit him again, wack!.

"Say what?"

"Keith is the one that shot you. But we all was at the house that night." I growled deep in my throat. The night coming back to me vividly.

"What been that nigga Keith got wit me?" I asked menacingly.

"Pat paid him to burn your house down and to scar you!" I studied his eyes trying to gauge his honesty for all I knew it could've been a whole other set up. I stored in the back of my mind that it was time to relocate. This nigga had come

174

right to my doorstep. It was now confirmed the nigga Pat had switched up on me. Not only had he switched up on me. The nigga even tried to pay to take me out. The war had begun. I helped Face up off the floor. He held his head where I had clocked him.

"What part did you play? I asked catching him off guard. I quickly brought the pistol up again and he cowered back. "Don't lie because I'll kill you where you stand!" I warned. He looked at me a long moment with frightened eyes.

"I was supposed to help burn down the club but, It swear I didn't do nothing but stand around and watch!" I studied his eyes for and type of deception but all I saw was fear. I lowered the gun and called for Diva. She eased the door open and looked out. It pained me to see the once feisty and down by law firecracker who was once Diva now become a ski high, nervous shell. niggas was gone pay.

"Come here baby "I motioned Diva over to me. She came and grabbed my arm tightly and melted her body against mine. I watched face's reaction to her healing wounds. I heard his breath catch.

"Who attacked my bitch? I asked looking at him closely. His head swiveled back and forth.

"I swear I don't know who did that!" He said stumbling all over his words.

"I swear I don't. He only paid us to torch the club and to fuck with you. I did not even know she was there and got hurt. I could tell he was telling the truth because he thought something happened to her the same night I shot.

"Go pack our shit up baby!" I said ousting Diva away. She looked at me but said nothing. Turning she hurried to the back room and closed the door behind her. I turned to face and I guess he saw the look in my eyes because he threw his hands up and immediately started pleading.

"Please, please don't kill me bro!" His pleas fell on deaf

ears. "Get naked nigga!" I growled I frowned.

"I wanted to lay my head where I could rest and be comfortable at!" I said.

"You can't get comfortable around here?" I looked at her dumbfounded.

"Did you really ask me that question??" I say.

"I don't think Pat did everything everybody keep saying, he did." My momma says.

I couldn't control the disbelief coming over my face. She was still defending Pat. She still believed the best in him. She wasn't around to see the look in his eyes the last time I spoke with him. She wasn't around to feel the vibes he was sending off. She wasn't in the streets 24/7 to see and hear about everything that's going on and being talked about.

"Man, fuck Pat momma! I talked to him. I looked this nigga in his eyes and felt his vibes." My voice had raised a couple of decibels. My momma looked at me a long moment.

"You and that boy was the best of friends." She began.

"Y'all need to sit y'all selt down by y'all self and work out whatever differences y'all may have," Momma said. She didn't get it.

"Momma this shit done gone beyond negotiating and compromising!" I said looking into her eyes.

"That nigga paid muthafuckas to not only fuck over my place of business but to fuck over me too. I was shot up. My girl was beat down." I shook my head.

"Now momma I want that nigga blood on my hand!" momma looked at me a long, long minute and then shook her head sadly.

"You kids nowadays…" she sighed and looked off. I knew she had cut for Pat like a son. Shid, I had once upon a time loved that nigga like a brother. I heard the scent door upon and close automatically and instinctively my hand went to my waist. Momma looked at me and I at her.

176

"That's yo lil girl, boy!" Diva said chuckling. I half frowned half smiled.

"That felt like some Exorcist shit!" I smiled rubbing her belly trying to make the baby move again.

"She been movin and actin up all dog." Diva complained happily.

"I know she yo child. Just like you. She can't keep still for nothing!"

"Oh, yeah!" I said and started tickling her sides. She tried to run away from me. I wasn't going for it. Holding her down on the floor I tickled her to she almost peed on herself. She jumped up. It was bathroom that connected the master bedroom to the baby's room. When she rushed into the bathroom and closed the door behind her. I went into the bathroom and closed the door behind her. I went into the hallway and got the roses that I had left in the hallway. I was waiting by the door when she came out. She yelped and covered her mouth.

"Aww she cry for, pee roses" I teased her. She slapped my arm and grabbed the roses.

"There's something I must say," I started, Diva was looking at me intently I grabbed her hands and got down on my knees.

"Listen to me as I recite these words to you' I said looking deep in her eyes.

My days with you have
Exceeded my deepest imaginations
You've been my rock
When I needed something solid to lean on
You've been the inspiration
That's been here pushing me on.
A dream is just a dream
But reality is tangible
Being with you overshadows all thoughts

You were my dream for so long
Now you're my reality….

I was looking deep off into her watery eyes. I reached into my pocket and pulled out the small blue suede box. Diva's hands went to her mouth.

"Will you be my wife Derica Natasha Franks!" Diva burst out laughing and pushed me to the floor.

"Yes, I'll be your wife, boy" she straddled me and we locked lips for a long deep wet kiss.

"mmm!" I moaned.

"That kiss tasted different." I said smacking my lips.

"How so?" she asked frowning I looked off in the distance like I was trying to figure the difference.

"I don't know. But it tastes like a kiss from a wife!" Diva punched my arm and we laughed. Again we locked lips. She adjusted herself on top of me feeling the head of her center, I hardened.

"Damn girl, don't start nothing you ain't gone be able to handle." I warned. Diva looked at me with deep longing in her eyes.

"I need you daddy!!" Diva moaned rubbing her crotch up against the hardness inside my jeans.

"Just lay there and let me do what I do!" Diva said beginning to undress me.

"Once I get excited, I cannot promise you nothin'" I responded. Me and Diva hadn't messed around in a couple of weeks. I had been allowing her to recover from all her wounds. I didn't want to cause her pain. It had been a rough couple of weeks. Everything that Diva usually did turned me on from the way she walked to same of the sounds she made sometimes she could just give him a look and he would jump on her.

"Let me have my fun!" she pouted.

"What the fuck you at my door for?" Pat said evilly

178

Champagne was standing at foor of Pat's apartment. She crowned at his chillness.

"I I I thought I could come talk to you!" Champagne stuttered.

"What's up talk!" He responded coldly not asking if she wanted to enter. She studied Pat's hard expression.

After all we shared this the reception I get?" Champagne asked.

"Bitch, we didn't share nothing but a few samples of DNA!" Pat started and closed the door in her face. Champagne stared at the closed door for a few minutes. She was about to reach up and knock on the door when she felt the hard steel of a gun pressed to the back of her head.

"Bitch you chose the wrong team!!" Before she could respond she was hit in the back of the head. Bam! Champagne fell unconscious to the floor.

…

I didn't even let the body hit the ground good before I was putting my fist to the space between the doorknob and the door. The door flew open and I entered quickly with the pistol cocked aimed and ready. Me and Pat locked eyes. Seeing the look in my eyes he immediately dove to the floor. Boc! Boc! Boc! I let off 3 shots. He jumped up and ran into the bedroom and slammed the door behind him.

"Don't run now nigga!" I yelled to the closed door. Boc! Boc! I I fired again 2 shots through the door.

"That ass is mine!" I kicked open the door Boom Boom! Befoe I could do anything else. Pat had reached his gun and had fired back. I ducked out of the doorway. I wasn't trying to turn this shit into no shoot out at the ok corral. I was just trying to ice this nigga. I forgot all about the kidnap and torture plans. I just wanted this nigga dead. The rushed into the room ready to rip this nigga. But he had the window up and was nowhere to be found. I ran to the bedroom window to see that Pat had jumped out the window and was running away from me. I watched as he disappeared around the bend of the complex.

"You can run, but you can't hide!!!"

Chapter 25

I was sitting in my chevy big body watching the traffic go in and out of the dope house that Keith sold 'H' pills out of occasionally. The only reason why I hadn't stormed the house with gun blazing was because I didn't know for sure if Keith was in the house at this very moment. I was waiting for him to show his face. I didn't give a damn who all was in there when the gun started popping. I just wanted to make sure Keith was there and got what he had coming to him. I was gonna catch that nigga if I had to wait out here for the next months I had my 2 pac CD playing and I was Patiently waiting to help the nigga Keith exit this life and enter the next one of the heroine addicts left the house and headed in the direction I was parked. I powered down my window when he got close I stopped him.

"Look out buddy!" I called out. He hesitated then stopped looking down into the car at me he jerked his head.

"Sup?" He asked even though he was a few feet away from me I smelled his bad breath and body odor. I flashed him a 100-dollar bill and asked.

"You seen my man Keith?" He licked his lips and smiled.

"Yeah, he in there right now making a killin'" He said snatching the bill out of my hand and taking off. He didn't even attempt to go back to the dope house and score. I guess he knew the catastrophe that was about happen. Do I go get at that nigga now or do I wait for him to leave the house alone so I can kidnap him and have some fun. I know he was the triggerman that shot me and damn near put me in a shit bag. I had no empathy or sympathy for him or his kin. In the seat beside me was a AK 47 while in my seat was a chrome-plated 45 automatic with an extended clip. I had come ready to do Keith, Bam Bam and whoever else was in touching distance and was associated with Pat, Keith, Bam and the whole bunch. I watched the traffic thin out, then I made my move. I pulled the car to the front of the house. I jumped out AK held tightly and jogged to the entrance of the dope house. The door was coming open as I rushed up the sidewalk.

"Rat tat tat tat tat" I squeezed the trigger and let the chopper talk. The guy coming out of the house head exploded. Brain matter blood, tissue and skull bones flew. I rushed into the house. A tall stocky light skin dude was leaning sideways with Blood leaking from a side wound. I walked right up on him and shot him in the head no questions asked. I heard commotion of people trying to escape the house. I hurried through the house and spotted Keith trying to make it out the back door. I shot his legs out from under him.

"Awww Fuck, Awww Shiitt!" He screamed in pain. I rushed up to him. Pulling the 45 from my waist I hit him twice in the head.

"Muthafucker, you want to ride on me!" I growled.

"I'm sorry man!"

"Bitch nigga you tried to end my life" Wack Wack!" I hit him in the head again and again and again.

"Get yo bitch ass up nigga!" I said kicking Keith in his ass. I knew he wouldn't be able to stand up because I had broke his legs with the first shots I hit him with.

"Awww shit pleade please!" He cried. I kicked and stamped his wounded legs.

"You wasn't beggin when you was poppin yo gun at me nigga!" I shot him again with the 45 in the side.

"Awww! I I… Awwww…!!" I shot him again in the hand.

"Bitch nigga. Shut up!" I screamed as I kicked him in the head and neck. I was tired of fucking with him.

"Sleep tight nigga and save a place for yo boy Pat he's comin soon" Three more shots rang out as I sent him to an early grave.

I put the gun right to his temple and popped off three shots. I was gone make sure he was dead I had no time for errors. No one will get a second change unless God himself came down and delivered it. I quickly picked up my AK and prepared to leave the house. I paused at the front door and looked out. I seen nobody, so I ran out to my car and drove off slowly. I didn't want to speed off and draw too much attention to my car. I looked in the rearview mirror at the house fading in the distance. I wanted to spark that muthafucka and burn that bitch to the ground. I wasn't totally satisfied because I was only able to ex Keith out. Bam Bam had gotten away. I'd catch him. I knew him and Pat would go into hiding but there would be escaping the consequences and repercussions of what went down. I'd follow them nigga's to the ends of the world.'

When I walked through the door Diva was waiting for me with a big smile. Suddenly her face fell and she covered her mouth in a scream. Her eyes traveled over my body. She turned and threw up on the floor. I looked down at my clothes and seen that I was covered in Blood. I had some chips and brain matter stuck to my shirt.

"It's okay momma, It's not my blood!" I reassured her and walked to the bathroom to clean myself up.

"Sorry baby!" I said over my shoulders with her being pregnant I know she was extra sensitive to smell, sound and almost anything.

"You need to be careful baby!" Diva said rubbing my chest. I had went in the shower and stayed about 2 hours. I made sure I cleaned every speck of blood, flesh and brain matter off my body. I knew I would have to burn my clothes.

"I am, momma," I responded, my arm underneath the pillow while she laid her head on me and rubbed my chest.

"I'm serious Infamous, she said lifting her head up and looking into my eyes."

"You got Keith, let that other shit go!" I looked at her and frowned.

"Listen to me, she said stopping me before I could even respond.

"Let them go daddy, we can't lose you now!" Seeing the look in Diva's eyes did something to me. But nigga's had violated in a major way. I couldn't and I wouldn't just charge that shit to the game.

"Now ma, them niggas violated the code. My heart is cold for them cats. All of them gotta be erased before I can rest and sleep easy!" Diva just studied my eyes and said nothing. I couldn't stop now. I put it on my life that I wouldn't rest until I took out all of the people responsible for incidents that happened to me and Diva.

"What happen if we lose you? How am I supposed to raise this little girl? She asked.

"You ain't gone loose me!"

"You don't know that!" Diva said with feeling.

"You taking that risk. If anybody see you and give the police your description. They coming to get you. They don't give a damn about them violating no code or none of that shit!!" Diva said, worried and afraid. I think it did something to her to see me come in with all that blood on

184

my shirt.She thought it was my blood at first until I told her different. In the beginning, I thought Diva was a thoroughbred gangster bitch. But it seemed that the concussion she sustained from her and her pregnancy had changed her.

"I understand what you sayin. But understand me." I began. "I'm a ganxta. Certain things a ganxta just won't tolerate. My conscious just won't let me," I said, staring at Diva long and hard. I really needed her to understand me and the code I lived and died by. She was gonna be my wife eternally and beyond.

"These niggas beat you baby for some paper? These nigga's soul was damn near bought. Every last one of them gotta pay for that!" I screamed as my angers poured out tears. This shit was all out war.

Chapter 26

"That nigga ain't doin no playin' he in animal mode." Trey said sitting across from Pat in the eating booth at the Pancake House. Pat was wearing a brace on one of his legs. He had injured his knee jumping out the window the other day.

"Ain't nobody fearin' that nigga!" Pat fronted. He failed to mention that the reason he was now partially handicapped was because he fled in fear. He almost caused his own demise when he jumped out of the window at the two-story apartment.

"It ain't about fear playa. It's about being wise," Trey was at a party the other night in Southwest. Infamous had come through. He had murder in his eyes and a couple of guns in visibility. He asked a few questions and made a lot of statements. He had basically warned the world. When he catch Pat and find the identity of the guy that pistol-whipped Diva. He was goin' apeshit. Trey had watched him move through the crowd at the party like a shark moving through bloody water. He watched Infamous' eyes roaming all over the place. He was studying every bitch nigga and bitch. If he met with any resistance of negative energy, he was gonna smash one right!

"Right about what?" Pat asked dumbly. Trey took a bite of his pancakes. He chewed and looked at Pat and Infamous was real serious beyond real serious. Pat was trying to look all cool, calm and calculated but Trey knew that deep inside Pat had to feel some type of anxiousness or something. The nigga wasn't as numb as he wanted everybody to believe he was.

"Well, Pat, I see that you really in over your head wth goin' at it with Infamous," Trey explained.

"You don't even understand the monster you choose as your foe." Pat said, staring him down.

"The reason you wanna beat Infamous." Trey said pausing for full of effect. "Is because you don't respect him." Pat frowned. He knew deep down that he respected Infamous' mind and gangsta ways. He knew that Infamous was nothing to play with, that's why he really hired the flunkies to try and get at him instead of doing it himself. Now he felt like a fucking coward. He had a gun and he still had ran. He had jumped out the fucking window. He could've broken his neck or anything. He had heard the door come crashing down. When he had looked and saw the look of death in Infamous eyes automatically he just took off without even thinking. He didn't ask no questions when the instinct of fight or flight kicked in. Something in him just made him choose flight.

"What does respecting the nigga got to do with beatin him?" Pat asked frowning.

"This ain't no game this shit real. It's kill or be killed." Pat continued.

"So when you gone kill the nigga?" Trey asked looking at Pat. Pat looked out the window of the pancake house. He watched the cars enter and exit the parking lot for a minute was he really ready to kill Infamous? At first he had been in his feelings about Infamous and Diva. He was jealous of the relationship they had. He had wanted Diva for himself from the first moment that he had seen her. Then when they had went on their criminal adventure he saw Diva on her gutta level. He was in love. But he had seen it from the onslaught that Diva and Infamous were destined to be. He didn't think he would began acting the way that he did. Sometimes, he felt he couldn't help himself. Something just happens. But now that he was thinking with a level head. Is murder how he wanted to play this? It was really too late and he knew it. He had drawn first blood. He had popped this off. Now he was regretting the day that he and Infamous had met Diva wasn't no going back now. He couldn't undo what was already done.

"I'm gone catch that nigga slippin and I'm gone get him and that hoe!" Pat looked at Trey.

"This ain't the movies you gotta be ready to clap on site." Trey said seriously.

"The nigga moved out of the hood. He stay somewhere on the outskirts of the city. Nobody knows where the nigga rest his head at." Pat complained.

"You don't need to get that nigga where he sleep at. You can get that nigga anywhere." Trey responded.

"This ain't no storybook war. Ain't no rules in expirin' a nigga. Fuck all that strategizing and planning when you see the nigga squeeze at him."

"I wish this shit never would have began," Pat sighed shaking his head. Trey studies Pat. This nigga was scared. Why the fuck did he fuck with Infamous in the first place if he was so pussy?! Trey looked at the conflicting emotions and feelings play out on Pat's face and in his eyes this nigga was a afraid of Infamous.Why the fuck did he start this shit then??

...

Champagne laid on the bed in the Hotel room her eyes was

puffy, swollen and red. She had been crying for the last 2 days. She hadn't eaten or slept. Her head was still throbbing from the blow Infamous had delivered to the back of her head. She had laid in the same clothes. She hadn't moved. The room was paid up for a full week. She had came into the room and fell on a spot on the bed and cried for forever. She didn't know how things had come to this how had things falling so fast.

Damn nigga's had always been the cause of all her heartache and pain every major catastrophe that had happened in her life had been caused by the male gender. That's one of the reasons she had chosen to become a lesbian. Now here she was again. Fucked up because of the actions of a nigga. All she had wanted in the beginning was to have a little fun. Get a little dick on the side" Oh my God! Red! Champagne thought. Her baby, her best friend, Her lover her everything. Now she was gone! Champagne rubbed at the deep tear on the side of her face. Where the splintered wood from the door when Red was shooting at her had cut her when Red had tried to shoot.

Chapter 27

"Man, this is too much money to pass up!" Diva looked at me coolly.

"We gone come out with at least 30 G's." Trey said adding more sugar to the sweet temptation. Who ever heard of a salvage yard having so much cash. Trey had come to Infamous old stash house. He had called Infamous had Diva drive him. He wanted to be totally unoccupied so he could focus and concentrate, He didn't trust nobody now. He didn't want to voluntarily walk into a trap He didn't have no beef with Trey. But shid, he also didn't have no beef with the other niggas that shot him and the ones that try to do Diva in.

"How we gone work this shit out? I asked looking at Trey. We needed a plan.

"Look, I already know one of the nigga's that works in the office" Trey responded.

"He gone let me know when it's cool to move."

"Who is the niggaaa?" I asked. This shit could be a set up.

"The dude name is David. His uncle run the yard. But they had a falling out about some shit so now he trying to get a little get back!" Trey responded. Somebody else turning fraud.

"I want to see where this place is and the layout of it all." I told Trey. He made it sound too easy and usually when something sounded too easy….

"If you want we can take a ride now" Trey answered. I looked at Diva and she looked at me.

"What do you think momma? I asked she hunched her shoulders and said.

"Its on you daddy. I think it'll be wise for us to at least see the place. So what better time to go other than now!" I nodded to Trey.

"Let's ride!"

We pulled up outside the large salvage yard. A big white aluminum fence stood about 10 feet high razor wire across the top. Over the top you could see old cars and car body's some of them stacked on top of each other.I directed Diva to just keep driving but to drive slow.I really couldn't see anything. But I saw that once we got into the compound. T was one way in and one way out.

"How many dogs they got inside?" I asked Trey. He was sitting in the backseat.

"They have 6. But they keep them locked in a cage in the back during business hours. "Trey explained well I knew one thing for certain. The drame was going down during business hours.

"Do we suppose to hit this shit while this Diesel is there or what!" I asked trying to figure out. How we gonna do this.

"Yeah, he gone be there. They got a safe that they fill up every four days.

"So we gone alert us. On one of the day cycles." Trey explained "so we gone have to hit him on the day that he chooses?" I asked I wasn't feeling that all types of shit can be set up. All types of traps could be set.

"Basically yeah." They answered I looked over at Diva. She glanced at me communicating silently.

192

"That don't feel right." I responded. Trey frowned.
"He turning us on to some money why would he try to set us up." Again I glanced at Diva and Trey catching on and reading our silent communication.

"I'm not out to get you. I have no beef with you. All I want to do to get money with you." They defended. I looked at Diva. I know she really didn't want to get involved in any more trouble. She was pregnant with our first child. We had come so far from where we first started. Before she had gotten assaulted. She had a thieving beauty salon going. She had been taking night classes to get her real estate license. She was only a couple of hours shy of achieving just what she set out to maintain. They had plenty of money stashed away. But the temptation of more easy money was hard for me to resist. I promised her that if we pulled this one lick of with Trey that this would be the last one.

"We in." I said over my shoulder.

"But..." I paused and looked Trey square in.

"If I detect any funny shit you gone bite the first bullet."
Trey looked at me long and hard.

"I don't know why you keep thinking a nigga out to get you." Trey began.

"But I'm tellin' you I'm legit with mine."

"Let's just hope you are!" I say, loud as fuck.

Back at our place, me and Diva for in a second round of acrobatic sex. She surprised the shit out of me with her energy and passion. Our love making had always been passionate, intense, and satisfying. But tonight it was a whole new different type of energy. I started off being delicate with her because of the baby that was growing inside of her belly. Bu, Diva had set the tone. Instead of me fucking her, she had fucked me. No, she was laying beside me curled in a fetal position. I watched her sleep for a while. Her beautiful black skin glowing. Her full lips partially open. I've only had known her for a short while, but it felt like we had been together forever. I never thought I'd want to settle down. Get married and have a family. Now, here I was. Ready to get on some "Huxtable" shit. I eased out of the bed. Careful not to wake Diva up. She needed her rest. I had made me a game room in the basement of our new house. I had a stereo system in with big speakers setup in every corner. I had made the walls soundproof. I had a large pool table setup in the middle of the floor. Since the only person that knew about our new residence was my mom, I had yet to play anybody, other than Diva, in pool. I had decorated the walls with pictures and posters of athletes and famous people I admired. I had a huge black and white painting of Tupac throwing up the "w" for the west coast. I was a southwest nigga tried and true.

I went to the stereo system and put in Pac's "Me Against the World" album…. "First fuck you bitch and the set you claim, it's west side when we ride comin' quick with game…." Tupac voice came through the speakers. Hearing L-Pac always gave me a unique type of energy. It put me in a zone. I rack the balls up on top of the table and got ready to play me a game of pool.

"I got nothin' to lose. It's just me against the world baby." I got nothin' to lose. It's just me against the world" after the last lick I was gonna take Diva and do some shit e nigga and never done before. I was gonna give her my last name and then take her out of the states for a honeymoon. Maybe to Paris or another famous country.

194

Chapter 28

"Bitch look at you!" Red greeted Diva with a huge bear hug. Red smiling from ear to ear look Diva up and down. Diva was wearing a maternity top and blue jeans. Her hair was breaded in two big breads. Her face fzt and glowing from her pregnancy.

"You look delicious girl. That nigga Infamous better watch out!" Red teased. Diva blushed.

"You look good yourself" Diva responded, and she wore a air-brushed shirt the color of a rotten egg. Skin tight jeans showed off full brick house figure on her feet was opened toe. Sandals the same color as her shirt. The paint on her toenails and fingernails had a similar shade of blue as the sandals and shirt.

"Now, bitch you the stunna!" Red continued. They had met outside Greens Point Mall. Diva had been out shopping for clothes for Infamous when Red had called her on her cell phone. Now they had connected on the outside of the mall.

"My fat ass ain't stunnin' nothing, I feel like a big ass water balloon." Diva pointed cutely. Red laughed and pinched her on the ass.

"These are the only things that looks like balloons on you."

"Bitch, shut up!" Diva said clay fully.

"What you callin' in?" Diva asked as they headed out in the large parking lot.

"I got me a green Nissan" Red answered.

"How far away are you parked?" She asked Diva.

"I'm right over these" Diva pointed to a silver infinite packed about 18 feet away from them. Red looked at Diva's new set of wheels.

"Damn Bitch What! You get a new car every other week or something?" Red asked looking at the new car with exotic rims, enviously.

"Now every six months" Diva said seriously. She had learnt how to start leading cases so she could switch up when the mood struck. She had learned the wisdom of leading cars from a chick she had met in her night classes. Now she had taken that game on ran with it! They made it to her. Car and Diva keyed the alarm off.

"Get in and I'll drive you to wherever you're parked" Diva said opening her door and getting in the driver side of the car. Red got in even though, she wasn't parked that far away from where they were.

"you got some where you need to be?" Diva asked.

"Now, I am a single bitch with no job. The only place I need to be is in a muthafucka's pocket getting chedda' like a cheese factory," Red answered causing Diva to laugh so hard she almost spit out the soda she had just took a sip of.

"Bitch, you wild," Diva responded emphatically.

"New wild is the west. I'm as serious as a murderer who is ready to confess!" Diva spit soda out. Red had to damn near beat her on the back to keep her from choking.

"Girl, you need to stop!" Diva said, shaking her head. Diva turned on the car so that they could get some air and listen to some music.

"What you have been up to?" she asked Red

"I'm not gonna lie to you girl, I been goin' through some

196

things," Red said sighing. Diva looked at her closely, she could see the stress showing on Red's features. Diva didn't know what to say.

"I can't believe that bitch Champagne," Red said shaking her head.

"I don't think I'd be too fucked up if it was some more pussy cause then maybe I could have gotten a little taste." Red smiled. Diva laughed at the humor. Red was trying to invoke in the situation mostly because she knew her friend was hurting.

"Then this bitch knew we now fire them" I'd!" She looked over at Diva." I'd" stood for 'Infamous' and 'Diva'.

"So she knew Pat was the enemy. I can't excuse that she slept with the enemy. Now she is the enemy!" Red said with bitterness in her voice.

"Where you stayin' at!" Diva asked.

"I got me a house on the southwest side." Red answered.

"I was thinking about movin' to the bloody nicked." She looked over at Diva.

"I think it's time for me to just surround myself with a bunch of gorillas." Diva studied Red, for a long moment.

"You know I'm here if you need me." Red smiled and reached and touched Diva's arm.

"I know, But you and Infamous got a baby on the way and y'all elevating y'alls game." Red responded.

"Y'all goin' legit and shit. I'm a gutta bitch. I gotta stay in the trenches!" Diva shook her head at Red sadly.

She knew that live and die by the code mentality. Ye use to know it intimately.

But her brush with death and her pregnancy had put everything in perspective for her. It had made her see the pointlessness and insignificance of the streets. The things that the game made to seem so important and glamorous. The stuff that only led to years of your life that Red would be pointless Diva had the same mentality not too long ago.

"We gone always be family." Diva said. A strange feeling came over her. She looked at Red and felt like this would be the last time that she was going to see her, without warning she started crying.

"You better stop this shit" she held Diva as best she could from her position in the passenger seat.

"I..I...." Diva couldn't even complete her sentence.

"Shhhh!" Red soothed. She knew that Diva's pregnancy had a lot to do with her extra sensitivity.

"Bitch you gonna have to chill with all the waterworks!!" Red joked Diva smiled.

"Girl this pregnant shit is tearing my ass up. I'm always cryin over the stupidest shit." Diva explained.

"Yesterday I cried because I couldn't open a damn Jac." Red laughed.

"I'm glad I'm not gonna let one of their niggas fuck me up like that," Red said twisting her lip up. That almost brought on a whole new set of tears.

"I'll be so glad when I have this baby it's fucking up." Diva and looking down rubbing her swollen belly. She looked over at Red who was frowning at her large belly.

"I love you girl" She said with emotion causing Red to look at her strangely.

"I love you too. And know that..." Red paused. She looked deep into Diva eyes. All of a sudden, she leaned over and kissed Diva hard on the lips. Then she got out of the car and disappeared. Diva sat there in the car for a long time before she finally pulled off.

Champagne watched Red enter her apartment and close the door behind her. She had been sitting outside Red's apartment for the long 4 hours waiting for her to return home she was staked out in a forest green Jeep Cherokee. She was fed been Patiently waiting on Lid to return home.

198

Champagne absently rubbed the deep sea, that marked the side of her face. In her lap was a small. 380 with a built-in clip. She waited a couple of minutes giving Red enough time to get comfortable. Champagne had altered her appearance with a long blonde wig. She had on baggy clothes. Under the hat she placed on top of the blonde wig. She had put on a part of glasses. She stopped out the car and looked around. The night was quiet and she saw no one in the immediate vicinity. She crept to the door of Red's apartment and knocked. She angled her head to a point just in case Red looked through the peep hate in the door. She looked around again quickly. As soon as Red open the door the gun was at her nose. Champagne didn't hesitate she squeezed the trigger. Pop Pop Pop. Before Reds face could absorb the 3 shots Champagne had turned and was headed back to her car. She quickly got in started up and drove off slowly. Her hands shook as the adrenaline lucked in. She removed the wig and hat from her head. She carefully drove back to the southwest. She had the music off and was driving in silence.

"You made me do that," She said out loud. Carefully checking her mirrors every second she allowed herself to calm down once she felt she was for enough away from the crime scene.

Chapter 29

"Where the fuck did that nigga Infamous move away to? Can't nobody find that nigga." Pat was sitting at the stop light in his Dodge Ram pickup. He had his phone to his car frowning. He had been trying to locate Infamous for over a month. Find out where he stayed. He had moved out of his apartment on the West and nobody had any information about his whereabouts.

"That nigga turned pussy" Pat said into the phone. He pulled off and headed towards the area where Diva use to own her beauty shop. He thought maybe he'd run into somebody that knew Diva maybe had some information he could use to locate them. His leg had healed and he was out looking for revenge. His pride was a little wounded and he had to redeem himself from that last encounter.

"He can't run forever. He gotta come out of hiding eventually and when he do I'll be right here waiting." He listened to the response on the other end and smiled.

"I guess I'll see him then!" Pot ended the call and made a u-turn. He didn't need to go inquire now. He needed to just catchup with Trey. So Trey was playing two ends to the middle.

…

"It's a go for next Friday." Trey said sitting again across from Infamous of their meeting place like the last time. The apartment was still empty except for a dining room table and a set of chairs. A bare air mattress was on the floor in the wondered room. This time Diva was excluded from the meeting and I made her stay home. She was too far along in her pregnancy to do anything. She wouldn't accompany us when we went to do the job either. It would just be me and Trey. I had now become comfortable with Trey. I didn't trust him completely. But I trusted that he wasn't trying to set me up for Pat. I was almost certain that he and Pat wasn't in cahoots to fuck me off at a prearranged location.

"We gonna go in like we tryin to buy car parts" Trey began to break down the plan for our caper.

"David supposed to be there by himself but just in case we gonna say that we're there to buy car parts." I nodded. Usually I was the one that planned and arranged things. I was the one masterminding licks. But this round it was Trey's show. This was my last gutta move. It was a major one at that.

"What kind of Pistol you bring in!" I asked curious.

"We really don't need no pistols. So I'm goin' in with this air gun that looks like the real deal!"

"A air gun!!" I found at Trey. This nigga was crazy.

"Yeah, we ain't gone have to shoot nobody. The only person for much." Diva began, "Aww Shit!" I thought I felt I wasn't gonna like what she said next.

"Matter of fact. I ask you for very little." She continued.

"But I have to ask you this. I'm gonna need you to promise me," she paused and looked me deep in the eyes.

"I need you to promise that you make sure, Champagne pays for this." Diva finished studying my eyes.

"Even if you got to do it yourself. I need you to promise that Champagne pays!" I looked at Diva. She was right. Diva never asked for nothing. Almost everything I've ever done for her. I did it for my violation. It would be nothing to get at champagne. I liked Red. She was like family.

"I got you baby. I promise."

On the day of Red's funeral the sky was overcast and grey. The forecast called for a 70% chance of rain. Red didn't have family so Diva and me had made all the arrangements. We paid to send her friend off better than the city would have. Due to the fact, she had been shot in the face we had to have a closed casket. The casket was Rose gold color. We had found a picture of her not too long ago and had it blown up. It stood on a stand on the side of the casket. A hired preacher eulogized her, a few friends from school attended. A few old girlfriends attended and said a few words. Diva wanted to get up and say something. I watched my baby walk to the podium. She was silent at least for a long moment and it scared me a bit. Then, she took a deep breath and began to speak.

"A lot of times people are judged by the way they walk, talk, and dress," Diva paused and looked over at the blown up picture of Red, which showed her in a halter top and skin tight jeans. She was smiling with a cigarette hanging out the corner of her mouth.

"A lot of times people look over you and ignore you if you don't dress a certain way or fit a certain type of description." Diva swallowed, I could tell she was struggling to hold her composure.

"I first met Red in Elementary school. I had on a pair of holly jeans and a too big T-shirt. My shoes was cheap and had holes. Everybody in the class was making fun of me and teasing me." Diva paused and wiped the silent tears that had slipped from her eyes. She glanced over at the picture and smiled sadly.

"Red had stood up and cursed everyone out that had

something negative to say about me. She threatened to attack anyone that said anything else to me. She then befriended me and taught me all the ins and outs of the game. After we became friends she would let me borrow her clothes or take me to go steal my own!" Diva chuckled. She looked out at everybody sitting around the church. "If y'all really was Red's friends, y'all know that the world has lost a beautiful spirit." Diva lost her composure and began to sob heavily. I had to get up and go get her after I set her down. I few more people got up and shared a couple of funny stories. Then we proceeded to the burial grounds. As I drove Diva sat beside me in the passenger seat silent and lost in thought. She was no longer crying so I figured she was all cried out. She had put in Red's favorite 50 cent CD. Get Rich or Die Tryin'. So as we code the G-Unit serenaded us.

"I smell pussy is that you Irv. I smell pussy is that you Ja. I smell pussy ….." This was also one of my favorite songs. Red was a gangsta bitch to her core. I had been missing her around us. She was always hyped and ready for whatever she stayed on some "Eve, Pitbull in a skirt" type shit. She was more down than any other gangsta nigga I knew. And she was loyal. That was the most best thing I loved about her. Because with me, "no loyalty no love!"

"You alright momma?" Diva just nodded her head without even looking at me.

"I got you too. On my life. It's on sight!" I promised, Diva looked at me then. Her eyes burned with an intensity I hadn't seen before.

"If I ever see that bitch while I'm out I'm gonna get that bitch myself!" Diva spoke.

I saw the determination in her eyes. I saw the anger, pain and the love. This was dangerous. I had to keep a close eye on Diva. That or I needed to hurry and hot that bitch champagne myself. I knew that if Diva caught champagne out in public, no matter where she was emotional and lazy enough to smash her. Pregnant and all.

...

I came out of the shower. I was naked except for a towel I had wrapped around my waist. Diva was sitting on the bed with my gun in her hand. I frowned at her.

"What are you doin'?" She looked at me with this peculiar look in her brown eyes.

"You gotta let me get that bitch Infamous."

"Diva!" She cut me off.

"I'm not gonna be able to rest or settle down unless I avenge my friend." I looked at Diva closely and I saw the determined look in her eyes.

"Diva you pregnant. Anything can happen." I tried to use the baby.

"I'm gone be extra careful. But I need to do this!!" she said with feeling. I knew I had to let her have her way. There was no other way I just had to make sure I was there when it all went down. I looked at her a long moment.

"Okay, But we gone do this shit my way!!" Diva smiled at me. She dropped the gun on the bed.

"Come here" she said. I was on my way to the walk-in closet to get some clothes. I turned and saw the mischievous look in her eyes. She licked her lips and beckoned me with her little finger damn seriously!

I had found out that Champagne was renting a room by the week at the Sunshine Hotel off of the Buffalo freeway. She had bought a small food closet that she was getting around in. I had been staking out the place for the last week. She had a bottom floor room in the front. Room 114. I was now parked about 5 doors down. Diva was sitting beside me. She had on a big haggy black track suit. It barely concealed her large belly. She had her hair in a bun with a black benny cap pulled over it. On her feet was black Nike Cortez's. She looked like a pregnant bandit ready to rob a bank. It was almost midnight and champagne was nowhere to be found. We were here though and we were prepared to wait until next year if we had to. Diva had a big desert eagle in her lap. She had told me that she wanted to cap champagne ass with something that would leave a hole in her body the size of a grand canyon. I had given her the option of the 44 bulldog or the 357. I knew she knew how to shoot a gun so I wasn't worried about that, She insisted that she be the one that avenged Red's murder. She have we were. There was little to no traffic tonight. It was a weekday. We sat in the car waiting listening to 50 Cent's "Get Rich or Die Tryin." I guess Diva wanted to avenge her friend while listening to her favorite music.

"I got you Red!" Diva said aloud talking to herself. I said nothing watching everything and nothing at the same time. At about 10'clock I was becoming bored and impatient. A pair of headlights lit up the area a few car spaces away. I felt rather than seen Diva tense up. I looked out my window and saw the Ford Escort pull into the packing pace. Before I knew what was happening Diva was already out of the car. Bun in hand, I jumped out and didn't even close the door. I had already rigged the interview lights so they wouldn't come on when the door came open.

Champagne was grabbing shopping bags from the backseat of her car. I watched as Diva approached her. It seemed like it all happened in slow motion.

Champagne straightened up from the inside of the car when she felt Diva approach her.

"Bitch…" I heard Diva say angrily before she raised the gun and began to hit champagne in the head and arms and everywhere at once with the gun.

"You fucked up Royally bitch!" Diva cursed Champagne

206

had fallen to the pavement and was curled in a fetal position. I watched as Diva kicked her several times.

"Come on ma let's go." I sad trying to break her out of her zone, assault and murder was illegal.

"Rest in piss, bitch!" Diva spit on Champagne and raised the gun. Boom! Boom! Boom! Boom!. It sounded like thunder had clapped. I ran to Diva and grabbed the gun. I knew if I didn't she would have shot until the cylinder was Empty.

"We gotta go too. She's dead!" I said pullin Diva away. She spit at Champagne bleeding body. Her head was in ribbons. They probably wouldn't even be able to get her identified by her dental records. Her whole head and face was a bloody mash. Diva kicked out at the body.

"C'mon 'D, we gotta get out of here!" I said dragging her away. Finally she snapped out of it and stopped fighting me and started walking with me.

"Go make sure she dead Infamous!" Diva said. I looked down in her eyes and was surprised at what I save.

"She's dead 'D. She don't even have a face or brain no more!" I assured Diva. I hurried her to the car. She quickly got in the car and I got behind the wheel. I looked around and saw that people were now coming out of their rooms. I had already had the car running so I just pulled off cautiously. I drove normally out of the lot and jumped back on Buffalo freeway and headed west. I was gonna take Diva out of town for a little while. Until after me and Trey completed our mission and split the loot. I looked over at Diva and she had this strange serene look on her face.

"You okay!" I asked. She looked at me and smiled.

"I'm way better now!" I shook my head and smiled. I had thought that her incident a while back and her pregnancy had changed and softened her up. Looks like I was wrong. Diva looked up at the roof of the car.

"You can rest now girl. I told you I got you!" she said. I said nothing. I knew she needed this moment. I just focused on driving without getting pulled over. We still had the murder weapon in the car. That was just one body or the later body to be added to the eagle.

Chapter 30

"What's up? I need about 4 of them thangs!" Pat said into his throwaway. He was trying to make a move. He wasn't completely dry. But he wanted to be ready just in case. No telling when there would be a drought.

"I need that good shit. Don't sell a nigga no dirt!" Pat said into the phone. He listened for a minute then he laughed. "Square bidness, you right." He listened again or a minute then responded.

"I'll be ready in 2 days. Call me with the location and time." They exchanged a few more words and then Pat hung up. He was sitting inside his apartment on the southeast. He had the apartment dicked out in black stallion leather and glass. The furniture was rented but he had no intention on ever returning anything. When he decided to move the furniture would go to whoever got the apartment next, or whoever picked it up out of the trash where the apartment managers threw it to. He had a stereo system in the corner with two large stand alone speakers standing beside it. Right now he had the Boss "Rick Boss" playing at a decent volume.

"I know Big Meech – Larry Hooker whipping work..." He walked to the back bedroom where his new girl was sleeping off the latest round of their sexcapades. Pat paused for a moment and watched her sleep. He had gotten him a short senorita. Her long dark black hair was spread across the pillow, where she laid her head. Even sleeping, she was sexy as hell. Pat contemplated waking her up and blowing her back out. She was laying naked on her stomach instantly Pat was aroused. Without any further thought he stripped off all his clothes. Climbing on the bed. He positioned himself behind her. The weight of climbing on the bed stirred her awake. She moved and her legs opened enough to give Pat the room he needed quickly he slid inside her tightness.

"Ooohh papi!" she moaned gripping him with her walls. She was already wet and ready for him. She pushed her ass back against him.

"Come on Papi, fuck me pussy" she pulled. Pat glided in and out of her.

"Shit girl" he exclaimed. This girl was a tigress. He started long stroking her.

"Mmmmm. Mmmmm. Me pussy feel good!" she pushed back meeting his strokes. She looked back at Pat with her slightly squinted green eyes biting her bottom lip.

"Ah Ah shit!" Pat exclaimed feeling the pressure build in his nuts as he was about to explode. She bucked back against him. Just as he was about to cum she pushed him off her.

"Aww fuck!" Pat cursed falling on his as she immediately wrapped her full lips around his 7½ inch thickness and swallowed his seed.

"Fuck fuck fuck...." Pat breathed in, gripping the sheets and looking into her beautiful green eyes. She didn't take her mouth off of him until she had sucked every last drop of his semen. When she pulled her mouth off of him she made a popping sound.

210

"Chu like dat pappi?" she asked smiling.

"Damn girl. What you tryin to do to me?" Pat said catching his breath. She smiled and crawled into his arms.

"Nothin pappi. I make chu feel good no?" she looked at me.

"You made me feel perfect mommi!" Pat said kissing her and tasting himself on her tougue.

"I gotta go make a play tomorrow. I need you to hold the fort down while I'm away okay?"

"Yes poppi!" Pat kissed her again.

"Now go brush yo teeth mommi. I don't like the taste of my own cum!"

…

"You ready to do this shit?" Trey asked. We were sitting at out meeting place. I was ready for whatever.

"I was burn ready nigga!" I responded. I was watching Trey's body language for any signs of funny business. I was checking the air around us for any type of funny vibes. So far I felt nothing Trey looked at his watch. "We should make it there around 4:50 p.m." he said. I checked my guns. A 9mm and 45 automatically. I had an extra clip for both of them in my pocket. I had 2 trash bags for the money we was gonna take away.

"Lets ride" he said. I followed him to the old school Lincoln continental we had rented from a smoker for this mission. I let him do the driving. I wanted my hands free and to be less preoccupied at all times. I didn't want no mishaps or to be caught slippin' at any time. This was it for me, after this I was done fucking with the streets. I was hanging my guns up. Me and Diva had been looking at projectiles to buy. I was already solidifying myself as a legit business man. I had gotten my DB license. It was also this other thing I was looking into.

It would allow me to start a corporation and get all types of loans. I wouldn't need a loan or any type of financial help after we pulled this lick off. But it would be a good way to wash the dirty money I was about to obtain. I looked over at Trey. He was driving the speed limit and was real calm, which helped me stay relaxed. I had the 45 fucked in my waist but the 9mm was in my lap. I told myself if the nigga make any funny movements I was gonna pop his ass no questions asked. We made out exit of the beltway. My adrenaline kicked in, Trey looked over at me.

"You ready I?" He asked.

"Strange time to ask that!" I responded and smoked. He laughed at my sarcasm. I seen the salvage yard coming up. A car was just pulling out. Trey and me looked at each other. He just hunched his shoulders. I picked the gun out of my lap and licked the safety off.

"No witnesses!" I said simply Trey frowned at me.

"It won't be." He pulled into the salvage yard. We drove into the compound. The office was only a short distance away. I looked around at all the cars. Some of them skeletons of their former selves. Some wicked up real bad. Some looked ready to be driven out at any moment. My eyes scanning all around quickly looking for anything suspicious. I was also listening to my instincts. So far so good. Trey pulled to a stop outside the office. It was a long trailer home converted into a office. The door was standing open. Inside a Brown stunned chubby man sat at a desk.

"Thais David" Trey said following my gaze.

"Did you tell him what we was cummin'in?" I asked. I saw David glance up and looked back down at whatever had his attention on the desk when we first arrived.

"Yeah!" I checked my gun again. The safety was off. I looked around one last time and was satisfied we were alone on the yard at that particular time.

"Let's go!" I said. I was not running the show. We both exited the car at the same time. I had my 9 in hand and Trey

212

had his air gun. We quickly entered the trailer. David looked up from the desk. Him and I locked eyes. Then he looked past me to Trey.

"The safe is in the back. The combination is 457-15-310-21!" He said remaining in his seat.

"You think I should let you tie me up of something" He asked Trey thought for second.

"That won't be necessary. But I might have to hit you in the head and give you a bruise just to make it look good." He frowned not liking that idea.

"Come on!" I said to both of them.

"Let's all go to the back and get this shit together." David looked at me.

"Shouldn't I stay up next and look and just in case somebody pull up!" he said. I looked at Trey.

"6 hands move quicker than 4. The quicker we move the faster we can be gone!!"

"Let's go !" Trey said and we all headed to the back. I glanced out the opened door and seen that we were still alone. I brought up the rear. Walking behind Trey and David all types of thoughts was going through my mind. Here we were about to rob this man for 30 G's. He set it up all because of some petty gripe with his uncle. When it was all said and done I bet David would be right in his uncles face playing the innocent role. Quickly, we emptied the big tall safe. It was only 15G's I knew that 30 shit sounded too good to be true. We filled the 2 trash bags we brought with us. I kept looking at David and thinking about the smoke that he had to be set up his own flesh and blood. Suddenly I saw Pat's face. While he said a few last words to Trey. Suddenly it sounded like Pat's voice before I knew it I had raised the gun and squeezed off 3 quick shots Boo! Boo! Boo! David's head exploded. Trey dropped the bag of money surprised. He looked from David's crumpled body to me. His mouth forming a D of shock.

"Get the money and let's ride nigga." I said grabbing the other trash bag with one hand Trey hesitated.

"C'mon nigga let's go!" I said loudly motioning with my gun for him to precede me. He grabbed the bag and damn near broke his neck trying to get out of there. I followed behind him, but looked ahead of him. If anyone showed their face they were dying today. We made it to the car without incident. Pat threw the bag in the backseat and I did the same. When we both got in the car he was fumbling with the keys.

"Calm down Trey and take your time!" I said calmly so far no one had entered the yard. It was around closing time anyway. Trey glanced over at me nervously.

"Why did you kill him, man?" He asked. He finally got the car started and moving.

"No witnesses playa!" I said simply. Trey glanced over at me with an unbelieving expression on his face.

"He wasn't no witness Infamous. He the one put us on!" Trey whined.

"If that nigga would betray his own flesh and blood. He wouldn't hesitate to cross us out!" I exclaimed. Trey shook his head and drove. He drove like he was in a 2 daze.

"There's only one reward for a smoke and that's death. All I did was kill a snake!"

Chapter 31

"Hey momma you enjoy your vacation?" I asked smiling as I hugged Diva. She was glowing and her belly looked ready to burst. She had on some type of top that left her belly exposed. Her hair was braided in some type of unique fashion. She was glowing. She had on skin tight jeans that it must've took her two days to squeeze into.

"I missed you daddy!" She said kissing me deeply. Damn!

"Shit! You betta chill girl before I bend yo ass over this truck right here right now!" She smiled widely and blushed.

"Ooh! Shit! You done messed up my panties Infamous!" She said squirming in my embrace. We waved goodbye to the family she had been staying with here in Victoria Tx. For the past week. I had to let shit die down and make sure calvary wouldn't come down on a nigga.

I helped her into the truck and went around to my side and got in.

"I got a present for you back at the house boo, but you gone have to be good to keep it!" Diva looked at me and pouted cutely.

"I'm always good. I'm a god girl!" she responded we both laughed at that.

"Check this out. I made a C.D. for you!" I said and pushed

play on on the sterio after a couple of seconds "R. Kelly's" voice came through the speakers. His song "seems like you ready!" come on and Diva screamed loudly damn near bursting my ear drums. She scared the shit out of me. I laughed at her wildness, Right after that Rome's 'I Belong to You' came on. Before the CD had ended she was in tears with her arms around my neck making it extremely difficult to drive.

"I love you Infamous" she said against my neck.

"I love you Diva' you are mine forever and always." I said rubbing her thigh with one hand.

"Did everything go okay?" She asked straightening up in her feet next to me. I glanced at her.

" I'm here ain't I."

"That's not an answer." She said frowning.

"It was only 15 B's and not 30 like he first said but we good."

"How much did y'all have to give Diva then?" she asked twisting her lip. I looked over at her and said nothing at first. She frowned and asked again.

"How much did y'all have to give David?"

"Nothing!" I said simply. Diva frowned.

Not..." I cut her off.

"Don't ask D." I glanced at her again and then frowned back on the road. I felt her staring at me from my profile. She remained silent for a while then changed the subject.

"So what's next?" she asked.

"We go set up a corporate account one day this week," I requested. It was time to go legit. I was officially retired from the game and the streets.

"You can start planning that wedding too," Diva requested and threw her arms around me, damn near causing me to have a wreck.

"Girl! You tryin' to kill us!" I exclaimed. Heart beating

216

wildly, she covered her mouth with her hand.

"Sorry!" She almost caused us to drive off the road. I laughed.

"You want to keep your salon or let Yolanda buy us out?" I asked. She hadn't been back to her beauty salon since the day she was attacked. She had let one of her best beauticians run the place until she felt comfortable enough to return. It had been profiting since she had been away. Yolanda had even hired a new nail technician who had the whole H-town fighting.to get an appointment with her.

"I think we should let Yolanda buy us out. I don't think I'll ever feel comfortable enough to return to that place!" Diva said and shuddered. I reached over and rubbed her thigh. "It's all good I think Yolanda will take care of it and do it justice." Since the beauty shop was Diva's first place of business, I knew it was her baby and would be hard for her to say goodbye to. It was a bittersweet departure.

…

"What's up nigga!' Pat greeted Trey. He was looking all rugged and unkempt like he had been awake for at least a week. He had about a week growth of beard on his face. His eyes had a funny glazed look like he was on some type of drugs. He shook his head and sighed.

"It's been rough." He said Pat was studying closely and 'something just wasn't right.

"What's goin' on with you Trey. You ain't lookin' good bro," Pat said searching Trey's eyes. It looked like he was seeing ghost and spirits.

"I.. I.. I gotta tell somebody." He said stuttering, looking at Pat strangely.

"Tell somebody what!" Pat looked at him struggle with whatever he had inside of him. Whatever it was he was having a hard time making a decision. He kept dry swallowing. They were outside of the Shell gas station. Trey kept looking around fidgeting. He then looked at Pat closely.

"Infamous killed David!" he blurted. Pat just looked at him. "Who the fuck is David?" Trey's eyes misted up and looked like he was about to cry.

"David's uncle Walter owns the salvage yard. Infamous killed David!"

Pat nodded his head in understanding. He had heard about that on the news a week or so ago. They called it a robbery/homicide. The dude David had been shot in the face three times by a large caliber weapon. His face and head had been a bloody mass of blood bone and brain matter. They had to identify him by fingerprints. The owner Walter had said that they had away with over 15 G's. Pat had thought Infamous was through hitting licks. Apparently not.

"How you know he killed him?" Pat asked. Trey looked away and seemed to be spaced out.

"How you know Infamous killed him?" Pat asked again, snapping Trey back to reality.

"I was there!" Pat looked at Trey closely now he understood why Trey was acting all strange. Pat eyed Trey up and down. His clothes were dirty and wrinkled. It smelled like the man hadn't showered in days.

"What happened?" Pat asked. Trey looked off again, his eyes teared up. It looked like he was about to break down and cry again.

"We was just supposed to be taking the money and leaving. But before you knew it. Infamous killed him!" Trey said and hung his head.

"David was the one that helped us to it. The money," He said shaking his head sadly.

"He didn't have to kill him!" Trey shouted. Pat grabbed Trey's shoulder and squeezed it.

218

"Who else knows about this!" Pat asked.

"Nobody!" Pat thought about it for a minute. Then he squeezed Trey's shoulder reassuringly.

"Relax, I'm gone take care of Infamous!" Pat said confidently. Trey looked at Pat closely.

"How you gone do that?" Trey asked. Pat shook his head.

"Don't worry about that part. I got him!" He answered confidently.

Pat drove through the parking lot of the Galleria aimlessly waiting on his phone to ring. Rick Ross's "Everyday I'm Hustling" was playing on the stereo. He just watched the traffic go to and fro. The females in their public best. He was watching the hypnotic sway of one girl's hips when Lil Wayne's "Hustler's Musik" ringtone sounded.

"Speak to me." He answered. He listened for a short while, a frown forming on his face.

"Seriously Morales bro." He said after a minute.

"I been in this lot ridin' around for the last hour waitin' on you!" He listened and sucked his teeth and shook his head.

"Alright fam. But you gone have to show me some luv on the piece for this shit!" Pat pitched. He listened to the response and chuckled.

"Alright fam. I got you. I'll be waiting on you." Pat disconnected the call and parked. Shit.. He might as well do some shopping and boppa-watching while he was here.

Chapter 32

Diva had received her real estate license and was ready to purchase her first house so she could flip. She had argued with Infamous. He had wanted her to stay at home and not do shit until the baby was born. But she knew if she just sat around the house all day she would go stir crazy. He was off somewhere now trying to buy 2 stick of T-shirts so he could get them printed on. He was supposed to come get her later so they both could go together and buy a computer for the house. They had turned the guest room in their 3 bedroom home into a home office. That's where Diva was now sitting. They had a Cherrywood desk that was at the time bare waiting on the computer printer, and fax machine. The rolling chair was cushioned and would spin. On the wall they had hung a picture of Martin Luther King Jr. Right beside him was Malcolm X she had wanted to place a picture of Colin Cowell up there too. But they had got to find the perfect one. She heard the phone ringing and struggled up from the chair. God! She was ready to have her baby. Her pregnancy made her fell fat and awkward. Every time she walked she felt like she was about to tilt over when she made it to the phone she was out of breath.

"Whew!" She breathed thin picked up the phone.

"Hello!" immediately she recognized the voice and it cause a slight dizziness to come over her. She grabbed the wall and stable herself.

"What do you want?" she asked she had slid down the wall and sat on the floor so she wouldn't fall. The dizziness had went away but she still felt funny in her belly. Her baby girl was going crazy in her womb feeling her anxiety.

"Infamous is not here!" Diva said into the phone. Then somebody clicked inside her head.

"How did you get this number?" She shuddered at his response as she felt herself becoming nauseated, so immediately she lay down on the floor. The phone clutched to her war.

"Please don't call here no more!" she said and disconnected the call. She had just at the phone to the side before the vomit erupted from her mouth. She threw up everything she had eaten that day. After her stomach was empty, she dry-heaved for about 15 minutes.

I came to the house to find Diva passed out in the hallway next to a large puddle of vomit. I rushed to her.

"Baby, Baby!" I called lifting her head gently. Her eyes came open slowly. It took a second or two for her mind to clear and the fog to leave her eyes and recognize me.

"What's wrong baby. What happened?" I asked gently she tried to sit up.

"Chill out momma I got you." I said soothingly helping her to a sitting position. I kicked the phone out of the way and leaned her against me.

"What happened?" I asked again. She looked at me and shook her head.

"Pat called." Instantly rage boiled inside of me. My fist clenched and murder entered my mind.

"How the fuck he get this number?" I asked then it hit me. Trey! That nigga was gonna die.

222

"Are you alright Diva?" I asked lifting her head so I could look into her eyes.

"I'm alright now that you're here" she answered weakly and helping her to her feet. That nigga Pat had fucked up royally now. I was gonna hunt that nigga down like a dog. When I caught up with him….

I helped Diva to the bathroom. I undressed her and ran her a hot bath. After the tub was full I helped her into the tub and washed her body slowly and thoroughly. After I was finished I dried her off good, and carried her to the bed. After laying her down. I took some lotion and massaged her from head to toe.

"Don't leave me Infamous!" she begged looking at me with sleepy pleading eyes.

"I'm not going anywhere D." I reassured her. She closed her eyes and felt to sleep. I watched her sleep for a minute and got up from the bed. I had some calls to make.

I was riding around the southwest trying to find Trey, Everyone I ran into said that something had happened to him and that he went crazy, some said he was now smoking dope and shooting heroine. I knew what had happened and what was gonna happen to him. I knew I shouldn't have let that nigga live after I popped David. I knew he would break weak. I gave him the benefit of the doubt when I should've just gave him a fatal shot at point blank range. Now I was paying for not making the right decision. I rolled over to Cherry Park. I had a hunch when I pulled up I seen Trey's familiar walk bopping my way. He was looking kinda raggedy. I pulled my truck right up in front of him, blocking his Path. Before he could react. I jumped out gun in hand and went to whaling on him.

"Bitch nigga you think this is a game!" Wack! Wack! I hit him in top of his head. He fell to the ground without a sound I stood over him and went crazy. All I could think about was coming home to find Diva laid out in the hallway in her vomit looking like she was dead.

"You gave that hoe nigga my home number!" Wack! Wack! I alternated from hitting him with the gun and kicking him. People were walking by looking no one tried to stop me.

"Get yo punk ass up nigga!" I kicked him in his ass. I was gonna kill this nigga but I knew I couldn't do it right here. Not with the crowd of people passing by watching. He struggled up. Blood looking from his head. His shirt was covered in blood. I made him got in my truck and I pulled off burning rubber.

"Nigga you may as well say your prayers!!"

...

"That nigga Infamous is losing his mind." Pat said to Daniel his jump off. There were sitting in her apartment. He had just received a call from somebody who had seen the fiasco at Cherry Park.

"This nigga beat a nigga in the middle of the road in front of the whole hood!"

"Who did he beat?" she asked not really giving a fuck but acting interested because Pat seemed really concerned about it.

"Trey. The nigga he robbed and murdered somebody with!" Pat responded looking at Daniel with funny look in his eyes.

"That nigga Trey want live past tonight!" Pat predicted shaking his head sadly. He knew he had inadvertently caused Trey's death.

He knew it was because of the call he made a day or two ago. He was gonna try to blackmail Infamous and Diva. Diva had hung up on him when he had called. He knew he had affected her. He heard the fear in her voice when he had called her. She had sounded like she had received a call from the devil himself. He liked the fear his voice invoked.

Now Trey was suffering for what Pat had made. "Fuck it" Pat thought. "You live by the sword..."

...

Pulled to a stop at the wooded area.

"Get out nigga!" I spit at Trey. The nigga had been moaning and groaning and pleading the whole rise. I guess he thought that would get him some sympathy. No dice! It was dark. We was alone except for the wild animals and insects that called this area home.

"Get on your knees nigga!" I demanded.

"Please don't kill me man I'm sorry!" He pleaded. I spit on him to hear him beg and plead only disgusted me even more.

"Shut up bitch!" I kicked him in the face.

"Aww! Oh God Oh God!" I placed the gun to his temple scowling.

"You fucked up Trey, all you had to do was take yo' bread and live happily ever after." I said staring down at his bowed head. He was sniffling and hiccupping.

"You had to go put that pussy nigga in our business!" I wanted this nigga to suffer but I didn't have the time or proper tools to do that.

"Now you got to pay for your mistakes. Save Pat a place right next to you!" I said Boo! Boo! Boo! 2 shots game over I turned and left the nigga where he fell.

Chapter 33

"Good morning sir" I reached out and took the pre-offered hand.

"Good morning Mr. Johnson" He took my hand in a firm handshake.

"Have a seat." He pointed to the chairs that sat in front of his large clutterless desk.

"So what can I do for you this morning?" He asked his clear blue eyes shined with intelligence.

"Well Mr. M. Author" I began reading his name from the name plate that sat on his desk.

"I just came into large sum of money and I was interested in investing some of it," I responded.

"How much are you trying to invest and in what are you trying to invest?"

"Well I have about 9,000 I'm trying to invest In what I have no idea that's why I'm here hoping. You could help me." I said honestly. I had been hearing about people investing money and becoming millionaires. I had looked up a lot of stuff on the internet. I had come across the name of this investment firm and had called and made an appointment to meet with McArthur. Here I was dressed up in a suit and tie and loafers looking like a professional instead of the hood nigga that I was inside.

"Well Mr. Johnson, you come to the right place," McArthur said smiling.

I thought about all the 10, 20, and 50 dollar bills I had at home in the safe Diva and I had purchased.

"Yes Sir, it's in a joint account at Wells Fargo," I answered. Me and Diva had opened an account a while ago after we had opened the beauty shop. We needed it so we could do the direct deposit. We now had a savings account that had over 20,000 dollars in it.

"Well Mr. Johnson there's many types of investments. I'll show you a few." He pulled a pamphlet from his desk.

When I left his office, I was more confused than I was when I first entered it. I was confident though that I had made a wise decision by choosing McArthur Davis' investment firm. I had his card which had his office, cell, and fax number. I was on my way to becoming a productive member of society. I wanted everything to be right for me and Diva and our baby girl. I felt good and comfortable in a suit and tie. I could get use to rubbing elbows with rich white folks. I wanted to be on the level with Bill Gates and Donald Trump. I walked and got in my new Ford truck. I had to get rid of my Dodge. I didn't want to take no chances that anyone would connect it with the murder of Trey. I had been watching the news so far and nothing on Trey, not even a missing person report was filed. I wasn't ready to get too comfortable yet. I knew I wasn't out of the woods just yet, no pun intended. The first few days I had been on high alert. So many people had seen me beat him down in the middle of the street and force him into my truck. I didn't know if Trey had family or not that would worry and notice him missing.

I hopped in my truck and checked my phone, for any

missed calls from Diva. There were none. I needed to check on her. I hit a button on the phone.

"Hey baby!" I said when she picked up the phone, she sounded like she had been asleep.

"What are you doing?" I listened to her response and smiled. Call Diva anything, but no one could ever call her lazy. She said she had been cleaning the house.

"Don't you supposed to be off your feet and resting?" I said frowning at the phone. The doctor said she was at the stage in her pregnancy where she was supposed to stay off her feet and do as little as possible. But telling Diva to stay off of her feet was like telling the sun a bird to stay out of the air.

"Well I met with Mr. M Author. I'm just leaving his office. I think we gonna use this firm." I informed her. Diva didn't care. Sounded like she was bored.

"Well, I'll see you when I get home. I'm gonna go check on Momma and Aunt C." I said hanging up, I started the truck up and pulled out.

...

"Boy look at you!!" Momma exclaimed smiling she looked me up and down.

"Ain't you lookin' all spiffy and shit?" She laughed at her own wit. She touched the coat of my 3 piece suit. Rubbing the material for what I had no idea.

"Where is Auntie C?" I asked looking around the living room after entering the house.

"She took Kristi to the doctor," she responded.

"Whose here with you?" I looked around the house noticing the silence.

"Nobody. Everybody gone." She sat down on the couch and I sat opposite of her in the love seat.

"Boy yo' name been ringin' around here and it all ain't been good either. What do you got goin' on?"

I looked at her blankly and responded.

"I been tryin' to establish myself as a legit businessman. I'm crossin' over and becoming a model citizen." Momma laughed out loud like I had just said the most hilarious thing she ever heard.

I frowned. "What's so funny?"

"Boy, no matter how many suits you put on or how many legit businesses you ever open up. You would never be a 'model citizen!" she said after she brought her laughter under control.

"Whatever." I waved her off and begged to differ. I was on my way to turning over a whole new leaf and establishing myself in the white collar world. I had just left an investment firm speaking to someone that was gonna assist me in my efforts. Momma would never understand. Despite her age and look, Momma was more gutter than any sewage drain.

"Where that girl Diva at and have she given me a grand baby yet?" Momma asked.

I smiled. "Diva's at home chillin. The baby ain't due for a whole other week."

"Good!" momma smiled.

"You better make sure that girl be careful if she lose my grandbaby. I'mma kill both y'all ass!" I laughed and got up preparing to leave.

"Well I just stopped by to say hello to all of y'all," I said I hugged momma tightly.

"I love you woman!" I said. She looked at me strangely for a long minute. She pulled me into another bear hug.

"I love you too… and boy..." she paused looking deep into my eyes, "Be careful out there. I know you ain't in the streets no more. But sometimes the old shit you done can come back and fuck you up!"

"I know momma, I'm good!" I responded by kissing momma on her forehead as I left the house. When I pulled off. I could still see momma in the door watching me drive away. I needed to come see her more often I told myself.

…

Pat sat in the car in the parking lot of the Super Walmart listening to Young Jeezy's "Thug Motivation 101." He was texting this pretty seniorita and waiting on his connect. He had been sitting in the parking lot for about 45 minutes. He hoped this wasn't a dry run like the last time. If Morales called and cancelled again, he would find another plug. He needed this because he was down to his last 2 ounces. He was waiting on a reply from the last text message he had sent when he got the call he had been waiting on. Lil Wayne's "Hustler's Musik" ringtone sounded.

"What that do Morales?" He answered. He listened for a minute.

"I'm in a burgundy Acura." He waited.

"Yea alright!" He ended the call and rubber necked around the lot until he spotted the Champagne colored SUV pulling into a spot at the back of the lot between a small Volkswagen and Chevy Malibu. He started his car and drove to a spot not far from the SUV. He looked around and didn't notice anything suspicious. Stepping out of the car with the royal blue gym bag. He approached the SUV. He stepped inside the SUV. Morales smiled at him.

"Amigo!" He called extending his hand for Pat to shake the gym bag. Morales opened the bag suddenly the doors on both sides was yanked open.

"Freeze hands up!" Before he could respond or knew what was going on. He was yanked from the SUV and thrown to the pavement roughly. He was searched. He felt the 9mm being pulled from his waist "fuck!" He cursed. He heard the policeman reading him his Miranda rights.

"Me, no Inglés!" He heard Morales kept repeating over and over. He was pulled up to his feet. He looked at his face

inside the mirror shades that the DEA agent wore. He
looked around and saw that a large crowd had gathered to
watch the real live episode of cops. It seemed like there were
a million policemen and DEA agents. 'Where the fuck did
all the laws come from all of a sudden?" Pat thought. Just a
couple of minutes ago there weren't any police around. He
knew because he was extra watchful. He hadn't seen a
single law car. Now there were a million cops. He was
placed in the back of the police car. He didn't see where
they had taken Morales. He knew that's who they had to be
watching and following."

"Shit" he cursed. He wasn't ready to go back to prison. He
knew he was a goner. Because they took the gun right out of
his waistband.

He couldn't lie and say that the pistol didn't belong to him.
He sat in the back of the patrol car and watch the other
people move around freely. His stomach felt hollow. He
knew it would be a long time before he would be able to
move around freely. What the fuck happened? Why in the
fuck didn't his intuition warn him of what was coming?
Maybe if he wasn't texting he would've seen something that
would have warned him. He played with the cuffs testing
them. He tried to slip his wrist out of them, nothing. An
officer came to the car and opened the backdoor to where he
was.

"Who does the drugs belong too?" He asked bluntly. Pat
stared at him dumbly for a couple of minutes.

"What drugs?" I answered.

"Wrong answer!" The officer said.

"I'm gonna try this one more time!" The officer said. His
voice raspy like he smoked 3 packs of cigarettes a day.

"Who does the drugs belong to?" He asked again. Pat
looked off.

"They not mine!" Pat said.

232

"That's not what yo buddy over there's sayin!!" He responded. Pat knew Morales didn't tell him the drugs was his. The law was just trying to trick him. Pat shook his head. "I know he didn't tell you that." Pat said looking the officer in his eyes.

"Try that dumb shit with someone else!" The officer looked at Pat expressionlessly.

"You right." He said changing tactics.

"Check this out. Help me and I'll help you!" He began. "You're an ex-convict, you had a gun with full clip. That alone gets you 40 to 50 years. Help me out and I'll talk to the DA and judge for you!" The officer said looking at Pat intently.

"Fuck you man I ain't no damn snitch!" Pat spit. Suddenly the officer's face turned beet red. His eyes narrowed.

"Now, fuck you nigger! I'm gonna make sure your ass gets the max!!" He slammed the door and left.

Pat watching him walk away angrily. A couple of more DEA agents came to the car a few times trying to get him to flip on Morales. They were after Morales. But Pat wasn't willing to turn on Morales. Finally they gave up and drove him to the county and booked him in for possession of a deadly weapon.

Resisting arrest and assault on a peace officer. When the magistrate judge read all the charges Pat was shocked. He knew the reason the officers had lied was because they were mad that he didn't flip on Morales. He also knew it was his word against the officers. His bond was set so high. He would never get out or be able to make bail.

"You know yo boy got you popped right?" 50 said to P.A. "What he got popped for?"

"A whole bunch of shit." 50 responded. He had got a call from a little shorty, he was boning. She had been at the Super Wal-Mart shopping when it all went down. She recognized Pat when they had put him in the back of the squad car. She had stood around with everyone else and watched everything. At first she thought Infamous was with Pat. Until she overheard someone mention that a Hispanic man had been taken to another car way on the other side of the lot. She had called lil 50 and told him about what she had seen. Now lil 50 was relaying the same information to P.A.

"You think we should call and tell Infamous?" lil 50 asked PA we thought about it.

"I don't know. You know they ain't as close as they used to be," P.A. answered.

"Where the fuck that nigger Infamous at anyway?" Lil 50 asked. They hadn't seen Infamous and Diva in forever. It was known that they had gotten married. Had gone straight and was doing good for themselves. They were staging some whore on the outskirts of Houston. They were fucking with real estate. Buying and selling houses. Infamous was selling T-shirts and shit. They said he had retired from the game and had gone completely legit. A lot had happened, Infamous had been shot. The butt naked strip clubs he had, had been robbed and burnt down. Rumor was, Pat was behind all of it. They said he even had Diva beat down. Well look like karma was catching up with him. If all the charges stuck he would be put away for the rest of his life. The pistol alone would get him something that would hold him for a long time.

"I don't know where they stayin' at," said Lil' 50 Exactly nobody knows. That nigga don't trust nobody no more!" P.A. said.

"I wouldn't trust nobody either, after all the shit that happened." Lil' 50 responded looking at P.A. seriously.

"That nigga don't even trust us no more." P.A. explained.

"Why not?" Lil 50 frowned.

234

"Shit I don't know, you gotta ask him that!!" P.A. said. He began to roll a blunt.

"I'm not mad at that nigga. I wish him the best." Lil 50 said shrugging.

"You remember them hoes Red and Champagne?" Lil 50 asked. P.A. thought for a minute trying to picture who Lil 50 was talking about.

"Naw I don't." P.A. said shaking his head.

"Them two dike chicks that was tight with Diva!" Lil 50 explained trying to jog his memory.

"Oohh!" P.O. said suddenly remember.

"Them thick ganxsta bitches!" P.A. responded.

"Yeah well both of them are dead. Somebody murdered both of them."

"For real?!" P.A. looked at Lil 50 surprised.

"They killed Red at her apartment. Champagne got killed at the Sunshine hotel!!"

"It's been a lot of killing recently. Sounds like they got a serial killer running around H. Town fuckin' folks off." P.A. said looking off into space.

"You think all those killin's are connected?' Lil 50 asked.

"Now that's some conspiracy theory shit!" P.A. answered looking at 50 frowning.

"Then you know that fool got fucked off at that salvage yard!"

"You right a whole lot of people have been getting killed here lately." Lil 50 said thinking deeply.

"You know who I haven't seen lately?" Lil 50 asked "Who?"

"That fool Trey!" P.A. thought about it. He tried to remember the last time he seen Trey.

"You know the last time I seen that fool. He was lookin' real fucked up. He was fuckin' with that needle!" P.A. said remember when he saw Trey the last time walking down the block scratching his track marks.

"Maybe the nigga done overdosed on that shit somewhere!"
P.A. shook his head.

"Man the world's goin' crazy. Everybody dying." He said.

"Maybe a nigga should take a page from Infamous book and retire from the game and move out the hood. Too much strange shit happening." Lil 50 looked at him sideways.

"Nigga I'm hood till I breathe my last breath. You gotta take the bitter with the sweet." Lil 50 said.

"You gotta be able to stand the rain," 50 continued.

"Nigga don't cry when the sun is shining so a nigga ain't gone drip a tear when the rain comes!"

"I'm just sayin" P.A. defended.

"Don't go kitty cat now nigga!" Lil 50 laughed P.A. frowned and swung at his head.

"I hope Pat gone be okay!"

…

Pat sat in his cell with his head hung low. His celly on the top bunk snored loudly. He had came in late at night smelling like stale cigarettes and cheap wine. Pat watched a roach crawl lazily up the wall. He shook his head sadly. He wasn't gonna be able to do this. He had to get out of this place somehow.

As soon as the lights came on and they popped the door. He ran out of the cell. He waited until the phones came on and called his court appointed attorney collect. When he accepted the call, Pat blurted out, "I got some information on a murder. I need to talk to someone."

…

I was sitting in the home office trying to figure out how to program the new computer me and Diva had purchased. Diva was down the hallway in the bedroom sleeping. I was getting frustrated dealing with the computer. I had been following the instructions that I read from the inside of the manual to a t, but the computer still wouldn't act right. I

236

needed a break. I shut the computer off and walked to the kitchen to get me a snack. Everything else was going okay. The 9,000 I had invested with McArthur and Davis had quadrupled. We had purchased 2 rental properties. We were contemplating dealing in commercial properties too. Diva's due date was passed only by a couple of days. We weren't panicking yet. The doctor told Diva to stay off her feet as much as possible. Her ankles had swollen up so she couldn't get up even if she wanted to. I was having fun catering to her. She wasn't too demanding. I was almost as anxious as she was to see my baby-girl born. I fixed me a sandwich and was on my way back to the office to mess with the computer again when the hall phone rung.

"Hello!"

"Hey Momma!" I frowned at the news she was relating.

"Oh yeah?" She was telling me that Pat had been arrested a couple of days ago. He had been found with a gun on him. He had been booked on several other charges.

"Muthafucker!" I was pissed. I had been waiting to catch up with him. I had some special plans for him.

"How much is his bond?" I asked I frowned when she told me the amount. So much for the idea that immediately came to mind. I was gonna bail him out and take him out, but now he was safe behind the concrete of the county.

"Thank You momma!" I said hanging up the phone.

"Bitch!" I cursed kicking the wall so hard a couple of pictures that hung on the hallway wall fell to the floor.

"What's wrong?" Diva appeared at our bedroom door. Her hair all over her head. Sleep in her eyes. I forgot she was in the bedroom sleeping. I had just seen all black for a minute.

"I'm sorry baby!" I apologized going to her and helping her back to the bed.

"The nigga Pat is in jail with a million and one charges!" I explained. She looked at me curiously.

"That's good ain't it!?" she said not understanding.

"Now that ain't good" I said looking at her with anger and frustration in my eyes.

"I wanted to get my hands on that nigga!" Diva nodded now understanding.

"Well now you ain't got to take no unnecessary chances." Diva said.

"Naw momma. The nigga deserve to suffer and die." I said angrily.

"Locked up he can find ways to enjoy life." I explained.

"That nigga don't deserve to breathe!" Diva looked me in my eyes and kissed me softly.

"It's okay baby. Maybe somebody will shank him and kill him while he's there!" Diva said trying to curb my anger and frustration.

"I want to be the one to do that nigga in!" I said Diva rubbed my leg soothingly.

"It's okay daddy what do they got him for?"

"A gun, resisting arrest assault on a peace officer and a lot of other shit." Diva continued to rub my leg gently.

"He ain't gone never get out!" Diva said thinking that would make me feel better.

"That ain't good enough momma!" I said looking at Diva intently.

"That nigga need to be croacked!"

"Come on baby lay down with me." Diva coaxed me down to the bed with her. I laid there beside her angry that Pat got arrested before I could deliver street justice. I had dreamed over and over what I was gonna do to him when I caught up with him. Now he was safe and resting in the county. Fuck! I cursed silently. Diva drifted back off to sleep. I eased from the bed. I tip toed out of the room I headed to the office and closed the door behind me. Inside I felt like this wasn't the end of it all. I had to see him again. I wasn't going to jail to do it I turned on the computer and went to the internet. I started researching successful criminal defense attorneys. It had to be a way to get at Pat.

Chapter 34

Pat sat at the table in the small room the size of a closet. He was shivering from the chill. The thin jumper offering no protection from the strong blowing A/C. After sitting there for what seemed like for hours, an attractive looking petite white woman entered the room with a yellow legal pad. She sat the legal pad on the table and sat down across from him. "Good morning Mr. Fredrick. I was told you have some information about a murder," she began.

"My name is Kelly, I'm the district attorney," she said by way of introduction. Pat studied her before he said anything.

"First I want to know what do I get if I give you the information I got." It was her time to study Pat with her cool light brown eyes. She looked at him for a minute then said, "Well I can't promise you anything. But if the information you give us about a murder is legit. I can speak to the judge directly that's over your case and let him know you helped us solve a murder. That would make them more lenient in your conviction."

Pat looked at her long and hard before he spoke.

"You know the robbery/ homicide that happened at the Salvage yard. I know the individuals full name that commit the crime."

To Be Continued…